RARE ANIMALS
OF THE WORLD

Francesco B. Salvadori

RARE ANIMALS
OF THE WORLD

Illustrations by Piero Cozzaglio

Consultant Editor: John A. Burton

MALLARD
PRESS

CONTENTS

FOREWORD

Man, who now finds himself responsible for most of the rapid degradation of our planet, must recognize that the world which surrounds him is not his own personal property where he can indulge in unrestricted exploitation. However, it is his home, and one that he must share not only with his fellow human beings, but also with all other living species who have the same right to life.

It is only by abandoning the mistaken belief that man is ruler of the universe and by realizing that he too is an integral part of nature will he be capable of administrating and managing the immense heritage in his care. He needs prudence, a rational conscience, and intelligent love, so that by caring for and respecting nature and its creatures *Homo sapiens* will be able to avoid the already imminent fate which is threatening him.

But mere respect and love are not enough. It cannot be emphasized too strongly that the root cause of the environmental problems, the extinction of endangered species, pollution, and all the other disasters besetting the natural world is the human population explosion. By the 1990s it is estimated that around one tenth of all the humans that had ever lived will be alive. And still, in most parts of the world, human populations continue to grow, demanding more and more resources. But although the expanding populations of the third world are a major threat, so too are the relatively stable populations of wealthy countries in Europe and the United States, since they have escalating demands for resources. If humans wish to continue to have increasing standards of living, then populations not only have to stabilize, but in some cases decrease. There simply are not enough resources to go round. These are facts long known to biologists, since the 1930s when it first became widely recognized how rapidly populations were growing, and the inevitable consequences of this. But by the 1990s it is almost too late. Even if most countries in the world were to adopt population policies aiming at stability, were those people to attempt to achieve a standard of living considered at the lowest acceptable in most West European countries, then the destruction would still continue. For a conservation biologist to predict anything but major disasters, both for wildlife and human populations in the next half century, would be to ignore all the evidence of the past and present.

The fate of the planet, and its endangered wildlife, is in our hands. We must do all we can to ensure its healthy survival for future generations.

"The beauty and genius of a work of art may be reconceived though its first material expression be destroyed; a vanished harmony may yet again inspire the composer; but when the last individual of a race of living things breathes no more, another Heaven and another Earth must pass before such a one can be again."

William Beebe (1877-1962)
First Curator of Birds
Bronx Zoological Park
New York Zoological Society

INTRODUCTION

THE IMMENSE VARIETY OF FAUNA AND FLORA

According to the book of Genesis "God said 'Let the earth bring forth living creatures according to their kind: domestic animals, reptiles and beasts of the earth, according to their kind.' And so it was. And God saw that it was good." This was the fifth day of creation. Later on in the Old Testament God issued Noah with the instructions: "Be fertile and multiply, fill the earth and instill fear and terror into all the animals of the earth and birds of the sky." There is no doubt that Noah's successors carried out these orders scrupulously. As the human population expanded, the animal kingdom diminished, with the irreversible loss of innumerable species. The lions of the great hunts of Assur disappeared as did those recorded in the feats of David and Samson; gone are the wild bulls of the forests of Europe, the crocodiles and hippopotami of the Euphrates and Nile delta. As if inspired by a divine mission, man has attempted to create a desert around him, both physically and metaphorically.

The biblical account of creation does in no way do justice to the infinite variety of flora and fauna to be found on our planet. Recent pioneering research in the high canopy of the rain forest has revealed that there could be anything between seven and 30 million species on earth, largely made up of millions upon millions of insects. Until then it had been believed that there were between one and a half and two million different species. The list of plants numbers about 300,000; birds number 9,000 (of which 1,000 are unlikely to survive into the twenty-first century); vertebrates (mammals, reptiles, amphibians and fish) account for about 450,000 species and the rest is made up of invertebrates, mainly comprising millions of insects. Nearly all the new discoveries belong to the insect group. It is therefore a relatively incomplete list of existing species; the number of species that have become extinct since life began would be impossible to catalogue.

EXTINCTION

Extinction is entirely natural, and all species eventually become extinct. Ever since life manifested itself on the planet Earth, species have been evolving and becoming extinct. This process had been going on for millions and millions of years before man evolved, and will doubtless continue long after man himself is extinct. The lifespan of individual species varies considerably with some such as the crocodiles surviving virtually unchanged for tens of millions of years. Others, particularly mammals including man, evolve and change with remarkable rapidity.

Within the last few millennia one of the greatest natural forces precipitating evolutionary change has been the ebbing and flowing of the polar ice caps. During the Ice Ages large numbers of animals became extinct, but at the same time, somewhere between one and four million years ago a new force arrived: man. Modern man probably evolved in Africa, and from there spread to all parts of the

INTRODUCTION

world. By about 25,000 years ago he had reached Australia, and 5,000 years later he was colonizing the Americas. In his wake there followed extinction of the wildlife.

THE EMERGENCE OF MODERN MAN

The idea of the "noble savage" living in harmony with the natural world is, sadly, largely a myth created by nineteenth-century Romantic writers and perpetuated by the twentieth-century Green movement. The harsh reality is that throughout history man has destroyed wildlife and over-exploited the environment to the limits of the contemporary technology. Desertification followed hard on the heels of the first urban cultures, such as those in Mesopotamia. Earlier, 70 per cent of the large mammals disappeared when the Amerindians colonized the New World. Once each wave of extinction was over there was an opportunity for a sort of new equilibrium to become established, but the emergence of modern European colonizing cultures in the late Middle Ages commenced the present wave of devastating extinctions. When the Europeans spread to all parts of the globe they took with them ever more efficient ways of killing wildlife: boats equipped for long sea voyages, with guns, harpoons, and nets. Then with the coming of the Industrial Revolution the process of slaughter and habitat destruction became mechanized and more ruthlessly efficient. Even the nineteenth-century destruction was to pale into insignificance when in the second half of the twentieth century increasingly efficient

technology was being harnessed to fuel an obsessively consumer-orientated society. Not only are individual species being exterminated, but also entire life support systems. Most important of all, the vast tropical forests are being felled at a rate which many people believe is affecting the climate of the planet. It is widely predicted that unless such devastation is halted there will be widespread climatic changes, which may precipitate disasters such as drought, flooding, melting or expansion of the ice caps. All life is interdependent and consequently not only is the quality of human life on this planet likely to be affected, ultimately the survival of the human species depends on its ability to control its depredations of the environment in which it lives.

MAN'S RESPONSIBILITY FOR EXTINCTION

It is clear that in recent times man, rather than any ecological cause, has been responsible for the loss of so many species: either through intensive hunting and wholesale slaughter, or through the destruction of natural habitat (deforestation, urbanization, transformation of the land for agriculture, etc.).

Ever since man appeared on earth he has hunted animals; for food, clothing, or simply for his own amusement. The effects have been disastrous for some species. Many scientists attribute their extinction to large scale slaughter on the part of our ancestors. Huge deposits of bones at the foot of precipices suggest that large herds of herbivorous creatures, particularly wild horses, were forced over

INTRODUCTION

these cliffs to their death. The American Bison suffered similar persecution in the last century. It is estimated that there were about 60 million head of bison in North America at the beginning of the eighteenth century. In less than 200 years they were brought to the brink of extinction largely because of gratuitous hunting. Armed with rifles, there were men who specialized in wholesale slaughter, like the famous Buffalo Bill, who killed about 250 in one day alone. Often only the tongue was consumed and the animal left to rot on the prairies. Hunting trips were organized on the railroads and passengers were provided with firearms to shoot the peaceful beasts from the train windows. As a result of this by 1890 there were only a few dozen American Bison left. Fortunately the species was saved from extinction thanks to the swift intervention of protective legislature and a growing awareness of the importance of conservation. Today there are flourishing populations of American Bison throughout the national parks of the United States and Canada.

The Passenger Pigeon did not have such a fortunate reprieve. Again it was hunting that was responsible for the bird's demise; there had once been billions. In 1855 it was reported that one New York merchant was selling 18,000 pigeons daily. In 1869 more than seven and a half million were caught in one area; in 1879 one billion Passenger Pigeons were killed in Michigan alone. The eminent naturalist, John James Audubon, described one of these massacres: "Already some thousands had been killed by men armed with sticks; but fresh flocks came without cease. One could barely hear the rifle shots; I would

not have noticed the shots fired had I not seen them reloading their weapons. The hunters stood in piles of dead, dying, or wounded animals. The pigeons were piled up, everyone took as many as he wanted and then the pigs were let loose to eat the rest."

The French naturalist Figuier affirmed: "These massacres are in nowise injurious to the existence of this species. In short, according to Audubon, the number of these pigeons becomes doubled or quadrupled in a single year." These comments were quickly proved invalid by the subsequent fate of the Passenger Pigeon. By 1890 there were no more important nesting colonies left. In 1894 the last nest was discovered, and in 1899 the last bird was seen in the wild.

Another innocent victim of man's irresponsible raids during recent centuries was the Dodo. This large flightless relative of the pigeon inhabited the island of Mauritius. Sailors who stopped on the island to replenish their provisions and stock up with meat would kill them in their hundreds. In 1589 Mauritius became a Dutch penal colony. Along with the convicts came pigs and rats which quickly destroyed the nests of these harmless birds. By 1681 the species had disappeared.

The French naturalist Figuier issued this damning epitaph on the demise of the Dodo: "The Dodo was a fat and heavy bird, and weighed not less than 50 pounds. This portly bird was supported on short legs, and provided with ridiculously small wings, making it equally incapable of running and flying, dooming the bird to a rapid destruction. Lastly and principally, it had a stupid physiog-

INTRODUCTION

nomy, but little calculated to conciliate the sympathies of the observer ... The Dodo did not even possess the merit of being useful after its death, for its flesh was disagreeable and of a bad flavour. On the whole, there is not much reason to regret its extinction."

These sentences embody the philosophy on extinction at the time when the most ruthless slaughtering was being carried out. The belief was that if an animal was of no use to man, or else its appearance was not pleasing to the eye, then it did not deserve to live. The same attitude applied to animals often mistakenly considered dangerous to man; this was the case of large carnivores. In ancient times the Asiatic Lion's territory stretched as far as Greece and Albania. Today it numbers only a couple of hundred restricted to a forest in western India. The tiger is also on the verge of extinction in the wild, as are many other mammal predators.

Often the reason man feels threatened by these magnificent beasts is the position they occupy at the summit of the food chain. Until fairly recently they were only considered to have a negative function: killing. Even today, despite the realization that these predators exercise a useful selection function by eliminating sick or weak animals, people still believe that they are dangerous, and are out to kill for killing's sake. They are therefore a threat to man.

But man is the real killer, armed with these unsupported and irrational attitudes: exterminating indiscriminately the puma, the coyote, the grizzly bear, and wolves with strychnine and cyanide. In North America the jaguar and grizzly bear were brought to the verge of extinction. The lions and leopards of Africa and Asia were decimated by hunting, traps, and poisoned bait. Wolves disappeared from Germany, Great Britain, Austria, Switzerland, Belgium, France, Denmark, Holland, and Sweden. The lynx went from Italy, France, Germany, Austria, and Switzerland. The last Barbary Lion was seen in 1920; the Cape Lion in 1865. Any animal that has in any way threatened livestock has been remorselessly persecuted.

Fashion has also played its part in accelerating the rate of extinction. Man's thoughtless desire to adorn his body with fur and feathers has become an industry more concerned with profit than preservation.

Many other factors have contributed to the impoverishment of our wildlife. The mania for carved ivory and ivory objects, particularly in the Middle and Far East, has drastically affected the numbers of ivory carrying populations (elephants, walruses, hippopotami). The serious plight of these species has prompted many governments, including Great Britain and the United States, to introduce a ban on all ivory imports. Strict legislature has also been introduced into the countries of the animal's origin, but the lucrative rewards for this illegal trade means that many poachers are prepared to risk continuing hunting.

Butterflies and shells have been collected assiduously, bird's eggs are removed from nests for private pleasure. There have been mother-of-pearl buttons, tortoise shell combs, and coral fashioned into expensive jewelry: all adding to the eradication of wildlife.

Superstition has also played its role by attributing powers to various parts of animals: in China, for example, the

INTRODUCTION

rhinoceros horn is believed to detect poison or restore sexual vigour. Musk from deer is also believed to possess aphrodisiac qualities and was widely used in the perfume industry. Also not to be neglected are the ethical questions regarding the collection of live animals for public and private zoos.

Pollution is also resulting in the death of many animals. Each year oil tankers spill their crude oil cargoes with disastrous affects on the marine populations and coastlines. Cleaning the beaches and coastline is a major undertaking and governments are now recognizing the responsibility of industry in maintaining adequate safety measures. In failing to do so they are liable to pay compensation for damage caused and for the cleaning-up operation. The sinking of *Torrey Canyon* in the English Channel with the spillage of 115,000 tons of crude oil was disastrous. The devastation caused by the oil from the *Exxon Valdez* in 1989 off the coast of Alaska was even worse; and the Gulf War has left pipes leaking into the sea for months on end.

Another killer which is often disregarded is traffic. More than one million animals a day are killed in the United States as a result of traffic. The flight paths of aeroplanes disturb the large birds of prey, and the destruction of badgers, hedgehogs, armadillos, skunks, and countless birds is plain to motorists the world over.

Insecticides are another threat to our planet's wildlife. They accumulate in the body often inducing sterility and ultimate death. Recent studies suggest that the alarming rarity of many birds of prey (for example the Bald Eagle and the Kingfisher) is attributed to the accumulation of chemicals in the tissues, which causes excessive fragility of the eggshell and the consequent loss of entire nestings. One of the more recent and deadly forms of pollution is the occurrence of miles and miles of drifting fishing nets. They have been cut loose in the ocean, and drift for years, entangling fish, dolphins, turtles, and other marine life. Sometimes over a mile long, they are causing untold destruction.

However, it is only relatively recently that the rate of extinctions has accelerated alarmingly and reached frightening proportions. It coincides with the technological advances over the last 200 years. No longer confined to limited areas, man is able to travel all over the world in cars, trains, ships, and aeroplanes. Today there is virtually no place in the world that is not being encroached upon by man. He is altering the landscape for urban development, harnessing the vast natural water resources to quench the thirst of cities such as Los Angeles and Miami, thereby irreversibly altering the habitat and home of many dependent species. It seems the more he advances technologically, the further he is trying to distance himself from nature; packaging his life into a more acceptable form surrounded by concrete and gadgets. He has invented synthetic substances such as plastic and polystyrene and the more sophisticated his lifestyle the more waste he generates. Instead of nurturing the planet as a precious life support system, he treats it as a dumping ground, unconcerned whether the marine wildlife in the oceans can absorb so much toxic waste. He is destroying the vast tropical rain forest which house innumerable species at an unprecedented rate: the less wealthy countries where it occurs are more con-

INTRODUCTION

cerned with the financial benefits than the global ecological implications. Roads are cutting through the ranges of many animals with disastrous consequences. As we approach the threshold of the twenty-first century wildlife is being forced into smaller and smaller areas of the world.

NATIONAL PARKS AND THEIR ROLE

A great deal of the attraction of wild animals can only be fully appreciated by seeing them in their natural habitat. An elephant in a circus or a lion cooped up in a zoo provoke completely different emotions and the majesty of these great beasts is diminished. Seeing them in the Indian jungle or roaming the African savannah is a unique experience and one that we are in danger of losing. The wild animal can only be fully understood when integrated in the flora and fauna of its natural environment. Zoologists and conservationists recognize the importance of the ecology sustaining the wildlife and they are endeavouring to preserve not only the animals themselves but also the framework within which they occur. From saving a species by placing it in a zoo and embarking on a captive breeding programme (in the case of Père David's Deer and the American Bison), they have moved on to the idea of conserving the environment within which the different species survive. National parks are the result of this enlightened approach to conservation. The first national park was Yellowstone National Park in the United States which was founded in 1872. The ever increasing importance placed on national parks has made it possible for many species to be saved from extinction. The Mountain Gorilla is protected in national parks that straddle the Zaïre, Rwanda, and Uganda borders: the Abyssinian Ibex is today safe in Simien National Park. In South Africa the Bontebok antelope has been saved from extinction. In 1931 there were only 17 remaining, but thanks to the Bontebok National Park, there are now several hundred and they continue to flourish. In Everglades National Park the Florida Puma can be found; tigers and Indian Lions are now found mostly in national parks; the ibex is strictly protected in the National Parks of Spain, France, Switzerland and Italy; and the European Bison, thanks to eleventh-hour intervention, is increasing in the Bialowiecza National Park in Poland.

THE BIRTH OF THE PROTECTIONIST CONSCIENCE

Until recently governments showed little interest in the preservation of the world's flora and fauna. Today a growing public awareness of the importance of the ecology of our planet has prompted political leaders to take a more active interest in conservation policies.

Public conscience was first aroused following the uncontrolled killing of birds whose feathers were in demand for trimming ladies' hats in the nineteenth century. News of these massacres (in 1848 500,000 herons were killed in Venezuela; in 1909 on the island of Layson, Hawaii, 300,000 albatrosses were slaughtered) filtered back to Europe and the United States arousing the indignation of people

INTRODUCTION

already concerned about these issues. At the end of the nineteenth century the National Audubon Society was founded to protect the herons living in the Everglades in southern Florida. One of the wardens of this society was murdered by poachers roaming the marshlands and he became the first martyr for the cause of conservation.

In 1889 the Royal Society for the Protection of Birds was founded in Great Britain; and in 1903 the Society for the Preservation of the Fauna of the Empire (today known as the Fauna and Flora Preservation Society) was established. To some extent they helped curb the ruthless hunting and laid down the foundations of modern theories concerning the conservation of nature. However, the societies lacked a scientific foundation which left them unprepared against the new and growing threats from the rapid development of technology in the modern world.

In 1948 an international scientific organization was founded for the protection of wildlife - The International Union for the Protection of Nature. In later years this became the International Union for Conservation of Nature and Resources (IUCN) based in Switzerland. This organization was vital from a scientific viewpoint but lacked financial resources to carry out research and conservation projects. It was therefore decided that a separate organization was required whose principal aim would be to raise funds in order to finance conservation operations all over the world.

THE WORLD WIDE FUND FOR NATURE (WWF)

In 1961 the World Wide Fund for Nature was founded as the World Wildlife Fund. Like the IUCN the WWF's international headquarters are based in Switzerland. The late Sir Peter Scott, first chairman of the WWF, described the four basic considerations behind their work as follows;

— that mankind bears a moral responsibility to guarantee freedom of existence for the animals and plants which share the earth with us;

— that the raw material of biological science must not be destroyed or allowed to die out as a result of man's interference with the environment, least of all before it has been properly studied;

— that the main maintenance of renewable wildlife resources can and should complement the kind of development needed to bring adequate standards of life to the greatly increased population;

— that the beauty and diversity of natural life should be preserved for its own sake, and held in trust for future generations.

We must hope that today, with the increasing awareness of the importance of conservation, we are in time to save many of our threatened animals.

THE EARTH'S HABITATS

This map indicates the different habitats in the world. In some habitats the number of threatened species is greater. This is because some ecosystems are very rich in flora and fauna, notably the tropical rain forests which are suffering mass deforestation. With the destruction of these vast life-support systems many of the planet's animals will disappear. The density of human population in other areas accounts for the scarcity of many species.

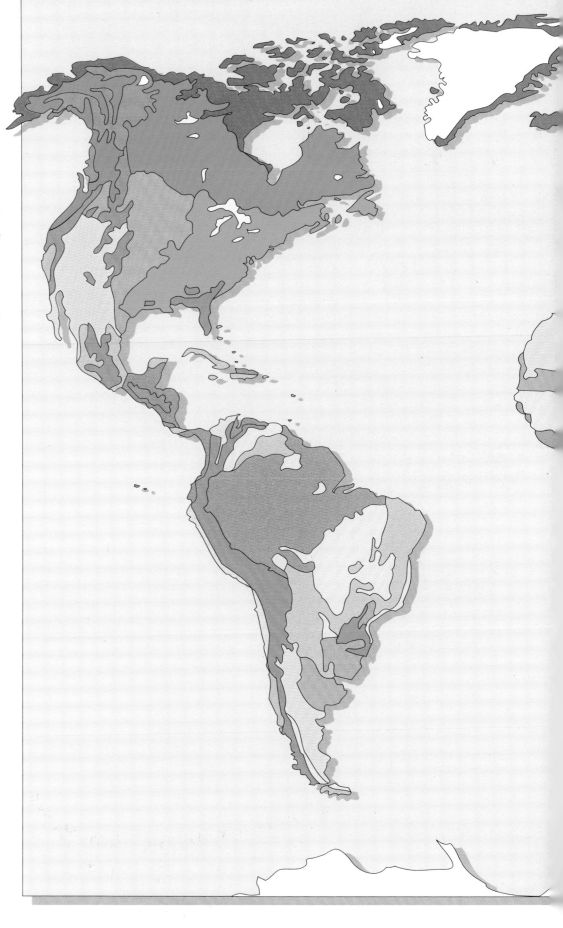

- Ice cap
- Mountain vegetation
- Tundra
- Coniferous forest
- Mixed coniferous & temperate deciduous forest
- Mediterranean scrub
- Grassland (Prairie & Steppe)
- Savannah
- Desert
- Warm temperate mixed forest
- Tropical rain & monsoon forest

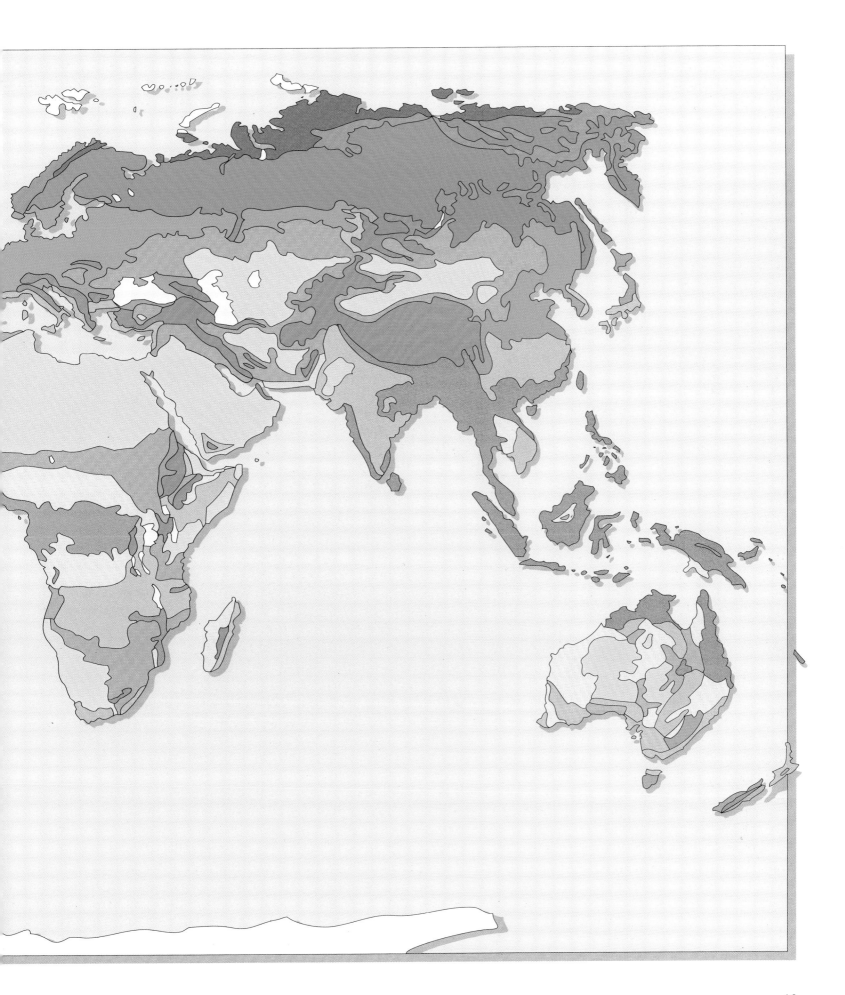

NOTE

The maps that accompany the animal descriptions show the overall distribution of the species.

Red indicates that the species is seriously threatened.

Blue indicates that the overall population situation has improved in recent years

EUROPE

EUROPEAN BEAVER

Castor fiber

Description. The beaver, with its massive body, is one of the largest rodents. The European Beaver is very similar to the Canadian Beaver (*C. canadensis*). The European Beaver measures up to 4¼ft (1.3m), including 1ft (30cm) for the tail, and can weigh up to 66lb (30kg). The hind legs have webbed digits for swimming; the forelegs, like arms, have prehensile digits. The ears are semi-hidden in fur and can be closed hermetically, as can the nostrils, when the beaver swims under water. The tail, shaped like a spatula, is scaly and hairless. It is used basically as a rudder or for building dams. The incisors are chisel-shaped, of continuous growth, and covered in yellow·enamel. The beaver moves clumsily on land, but is an agile swimmer. It feeds on reeds, shoots and waterlily roots in summer and fresh bark in winter.

Geographic distribution. Originally spread all over Europe east of the Pyrenees and a good part of central-northern Asia.

Habitat. Wooded flats by rivers and lakes. They build their lodges in the banks with two to five openings under water. In dry periods, the beavers build dams – using logs gnawed with their teeth, stones and mud – to prevent the water falling below the level of their entrance holes.

Population. The European Beaver, although no longer in danger of extinction, has been greatly reduced in numbers as a result of being hunted for its valuable fur. The populations in the various countries numbered only hundreds in the 1970s. European Beavers were recently reintroduced into Switzerland where they had been extinct since 1820, and they are being re-established in many other parts of Europe.

ABRUZZO CHAMOIS

Rupicapra rupicapra ornata

CLASS
Mammals

SUBCLASS
Eutheria

ORDER
Artiodactyla

SUBORDER
Ruminantia

FAMILY
Bovidae

SUBFAMILY
Caprinae

GENUS
Rupicapra

Description. The Abruzzo Chamois is a subspecies of the Alpine Chamois (*Rupicapra rupicapra*). It has a shoulder height of 28in (70cm) and can weigh up to 110lb (56kg). Both sexes have horns which grow up to 10in (20cm) long. The Abruzzo Chamois is distinguishable from the Alpine Chamois, particularly in winter, by a light band bordered by dark stripes which meet on the chest. This is the characteristic from which it derives it name *ornata*. The horns are also larger and more hooked at the end. One young (sometimes two, very rarely three) are born in May – June after a gestation period of 6 months. Chamois live for up to 22 years.

Geographic distribution. Until the nineteenth century the Abruzzo Chamois inhabited the high peaks of the Apennine Chain in Italy. The last individual on the Gran Sasso was killed in 1890. Today it is restricted to a few of the most inaccessible parts of the Abruzzo National Park and in the adjacent mountains.

Habitat. In summer it prefers the high, north-facing peaks where there is tender grass. During the rest of the year the herd, about 15 – 30 females and young, move down to the sunny slopes. Male adults live apart except in the mating period. In winter the herds descend to the woods and valleys where they eat lichen, moss, pine kernels, and bark.

Population. The Abruzzo Chamois is considered virtually safe in the Abruzzo National Park, established in 1922. By 1913 there were only between 15 and 20 left due to intensive hunting. By the early 1970s numbers had increased to between 150 and 200. By the 1980s there were around 400 and it is now essential to reintroduce groups to other areas of its former range to guarantee its survival should anything befall the original nucleus.

CLASS
Mammals

SUBCLASS
Eutheria

ORDER
Carnivora

SUBORDER
Fissipedia

FAMILY
Ursidae

SUBFAMILY
Ursinae

GENUS
Ursus

ABRUZZO BROWN BEAR

Ursus arctos marsicanus

Description. Brown Bears vary considerably in size. Adult males can measure 5 - 6ft (1.50 - 1.89m) and can weigh up to 1,720lb (780kg). Compared to other members of this species, such as Grizzly Bears, Abruzzo Brown Bears tend to be on the smaller size. This is possibly due to the isolation of this population from other Brown Bears beyond the Alps in Northern Europe. Like other bears, the Brown Bear is omnivorous: its diet varies with the seasons and it will eat fruit, berries, roots, small mammals, birds, eggs, and fish. The mating season is in spring and summer: the gestation period lasts between six and nine months. Usually two offspring are born in December-January when the female has already retired to her den for the winter. Brown Bears live for up to 30 years in the wild; in captivity they have been known to live for over 45 years.

Geographic distribution. It is found in the Abruzzi, a region in central Italy – a large area has now become the Abruzzo National Park.

Habitat. According to research carried out by the Italian branch of the WWF, the Abruzzo Brown Bear moves from one habitat to another depending on the time of year and availability of food. During the cold winter months they seek refuge mainly at the foot of mountains where they are sheltered from the harsh climate. During their migratory period they move up towards the higher peaks where they spend the warm summer months. Each area has a specific flora: forest and dense undergrowth, and grassland. Research has also shown that these bears tend to have their dens in south-east facing areas. Migration from one area to another – particularly in autumn when food is becoming scarce – forces the animals to seek food in cultivated areas, often where livestock is present.

Population. In the mid 1970s the Abruzzo Brown Bear population in the Abruzzi was estimated at around 100, and continuing to decline. In an attempt to halt this decline and also to reduce predation on domestic livestock, in 1974 a programme of reintroduction of prey species was instigated with the release of deer. However, by 1979 the Italian population was estimated to be possibly as few as 10 individuals. Elsewhere in western Europe the Brown Bear is barely surviving. There are small isolated populations in the Pyrenees (France and Spain), and Picos de Europa (Spain). However, the Scandinavian populations are not endangered and there are several fairly healthy populations in Eastern Europe, in Poland, Yugoslavia, Czechoslovakia, and Romania.

CLASS
Mammals

SUBCLASS
Eutheria

ORDER
Carnivora

SUBORDER
Fissipedia

FAMILY
Felidae

SUBFAMILY
Felidinae

GENUS
Felis

SPANISH LYNX
Felis lynx pardina

Description. This subspecies does not differ greatly from the common or European Lynx. The Spanish Lynx grows to a length of 3ft (1m), including a 6-in (15-cm) tail. The shoulder height is about 2ft (70cm). The coat markings are similar to the Caucasian Lynx (*Felis lynx orientalis*), but more prominent. The lynx takes its name from Linceus who according to Greek mythology was gifted with such sharp sight he could see through opaque objects. Experiments have proved that a lynx can distinguish a mouse at 250ft (75m), a rabbit at 980ft (300m) and a roebuck at 1,650ft (500m). The tufts of hair on its ears help the animal to detect sources of sound; without them its hearing capacity is greatly reduced. The edges of its feet are covered in long thick hair which facilitates movement through snow. This feline is generally solitary and hunts alone in territory defined by its urine, droppings, and scratch marks on the bark of trees. Lynxes prefer to hunt their prey − small- and medium-sized mammals, birds, reptiles and amphibians − at twilight. During the mating season the female leaves her territory in search of a male. The gestation period is 65 − 75 days; between one and four cubs are born. In the wild the male reaches sexual maturity at about two and a half to three years, and the female by two years; in captivity sexual maturity is achieved at an earlier age.

Geographic distribution. Until recently the Spanish Lynx was common; today it is confined to Spain. Its distribution there is limited to the Sierra Morena, the Sierra de Guadalupe, the Monte de Toledo and the "Marismas de Guadalquivir," the marshes at the mouth of the River Gadalquivir. A small number may possibly live in Portugal.

Habitat. This feline, the largest of the western Mediterranean fauna, prefers mainly mountainous areas covered with vegetation; maquis or "Mediterranean forest," composed of such trees as the home oak and cork tree, and dense undergrowth of arbutus, lentisk, and juniper bushes. Various factors have contributed to the decline of this animal: the sharp decrease in rabbits after the 1960 myxomatosis epidemic and the reafforestation of the mountain areas of Spain with a different type of vegetation. The animal has thus been forced to live in more open and less protected regions, where it is more easy to hunt and trap. Only on the flat lands of the Guadalquivir marshes has the Spanish Lynx been able to find a safe refuge. The few that have escaped are now carefully protected and studied in the Doñana National Park.

Population. The total population is virtually unknown; it is calculated that about 30 inhabit the Coto Doñana National Park. It is believed that the animal is extinct in most, if not all, of its former range. Hunted until recently, either for its skin or because it was considered harmful, the Spanish Lynx is today approaching extinction and there is great concern for the fate of the last survivors. The Coto Doñana is threatened by hotel developments. Other populations in Europe are spreading, and reintroductions have been successful in Switzerland.

CLASS
Mammals

SUBCLASS
Eutheria

ORDER
Artiodactyla

SUBORDER
Ruminantia

FAMILY
Cervidae

SUBFAMILY
Cervinae

GENUS
Cervus

CORSICAN RED DEER

Cervus elaphus corsicanus

Description. The species *Cervus elaphus* comprises 23 subspecies, five of which are threatened. Among these the Corsican Red Deer is in the most perilous situation. It is similar to the Barbary Deer (*Cervus elaphus barbarus*) from Algeria and Tunisia, which is also threatened. The similarity with North African deer is also found in several other species on Sardinia. The Corsican Red Deer is considered to be one of the smallest of the 23 subspecies. Its antlers rarely exceed 30in (75cm) in length and 28in (70cm) across. The coat is usually darker than that of any of the other smaller deer: it is brown in summer and becomes almost black in winter. Deer are gregarious animals and each group remains within a defined territory from which it rarely wanders. For the majority of the year the two sexes, stags and hinds, live in separate herds. In July, when the antlers are fully grown, the male herds break up. From this time on battles are waged between the stags. Sometimes they are just skirmishes, but they become more serious as the mating season approaches. This is during August and September when the antlers have burst out of their velvet covering. Once the battles have been waged, the stags emit a raucous cry, or bell, and gather a "harem" about them. In the first half of October, when their sexual appetites have been satisfied, they leave the hinds and go off alone in search of richer food to restore their strength. They join up to form herds again at the onset of winter. After a gestation period of between 230 and 240 days, a single fawn is born in May – June. The year-old fawns born the previous year are forced to leave their mothers. Deer generally feed in the morning or late afternoon; they are browsing animals and their food consists of grasses and tree leaves.

Geographic distribution. The Corsican Red Deer was once equally distributed throughout Corsica and Sardinia. It now only exists in two regions in Sardinia: Settefratelli and Capoterra, east and west of Cagliari respectively. It is possible that a third group exists on the Costa Verde.

Habitat. Mediterranean shrubland, meadows, and conifer woods.

Population. The so-called Corsican Red Deer is extinct on Corsica and only survives in small numbers on Sardinia; however, Red Deer are widespread and abundant in many other parts of the world and the characteristic often thought to be so distinctive in some subspecies may be largely the result of their environment. Red Deer introduced into New Zealand have developed into massive animals often with exceptional antlers. This is almost certainly the result of the lush, abundant food supplies.

CLASS
Mammals

SUBCLASS
Eutheria

ORDER
Artiodactyla

SUBORDER
Ruminantia

FAMILY
Bovidae

SUBFAMILY
Bovinae

GENUS
Bison

EUROPEAN BISON
Bison bonasus

Description. The European Bison or Wisent is the only representative of the genus *Bison*, which is represented in America by the American Bison (*Bison bison*). Until the 1920s there were two subspecies of the European Bison: the Caucasian Bison (*Bison b. caucasicus*), which inhabited mountainous regions and became extinct in 1927, and the Wood Bison (*Bison b. bonasus*, illustrated opposite), which inhabits plains, and still exists today. It can reach very large proportions: over 11½ft (3.5m) in length, excluding tail, standing 6½ft (2m) tall, and weighing one ton. They have humped shoulders and a brown shaggy coat which is longer around the neck and shoulders. It is gregarious and lives in large herds. During the mating season these split into smaller groups of about a dozen, led by an older female. In winter and spring they regroup again in large herds, except for the elderly males who live in a separate group. Both bulls and cows reach sexual maturity by two years, but bulls are six or seven years old before they are fully grown. It lives for up to 23 years, and in captivity may live for up to 27 years. The gestation period lasts nine months and the newborn calf weighs about 88lb (40kg). It is suckled for six to seven months but begins to graze after only one month.

Geographic distribution. Once widespread over the whole of Europe, it is now found mainly on reserves. In 1956 a number were released into the Bialowiecza Forest in Poland where they have continued to flourish.

Habitat. Tree-covered plains where it finds grasses, shrubs, and trees.

Population. No longer considered endangered, the European Bison now exists in sufficient numbers as to be considered safe. By 1975 the total population had reached 1,500 and it has continued to grow slowly. By the mid 1980s there were over 1,500 in captivity in zoos, wildlife parks, etc., and a further 1,400 free-ranging in semi-wild conditions in the Bialowiecza Forest and other protected areas mainly in Poland and the Soviet Union.

AUDOUIN'S GULL
Larus audouinii

CLASS
Aves

SUBCLASS
Neornithes

ORDER
Charadriiformes

FAMILY
Laridae

GENUS
Larus

Description. Audouin's Gull is distinguished from other gulls by the transverse black band across its red beak, its white head, and black wing tips. In adults the tip of the beak is yellow: in young the beak is entirely yellow with the characteristic black marking. Its total length reaches 20in (50cm) and the wings are 16in (40cm). Although the behaviour of Audouin's Gull is similar to other gulls, it prefers the high sea where it feeds on small fish. It nests in colonies on the rocky coastlines of uninhabited islands. During the nesting period and the rearing of the young the parents do not venture far from their base. Only when the fledglings are able to fly away themselves do the parents set off with them to the open sea.

Geographic distribution. Colonies have been noted on the islands off Morocco, on Corsica, Sardinia, Cyprus, and throughout the Aegean. In winter it extends its territory as far as Agadir on the Atlantic coast of Morocco.

Habitat. During the nesting season, the coasts of uninhabited rocky islands; during the rest of the year, the open sea away from the coast.

Population. Estimated to be between 5,000 and 6,000 pairs. The progressive decline is attributed primarily to competition from other gulls, such as the Herring Gull, which is less timid, and more adaptable when their nesting grounds are invaded by tourists. Audouin's Gull has also been attacked by fishermen who take the eggs and fledglings for food. It is now protected throughout most of its range.

OLM
Proteus anguinus

CLASS
Amphibia

SUBCLASS
Urodelomorpha

ORDER
Caudata

SUBORDER
Salamandroidea

FAMILY
Proteidae

GENUS
Proteus

Description. The Olm is a very strange looking creature because of its eel-shaped body which is uniformly white. The elongated head has small eyes concealed by the skin; there are reddish feathery gills on either side of the neck. The forefeet have three toes, the back legs have two. The Olm is adapted to life in caves. It feeds on small crustaceans and molluscs from the bottom of underground streams. Study of the Olm in captivity has shown there is an elaborate courtship ritual. The Olm can reproduce either oviparously or viviparously. The female lays 10 - 70 eggs, fixing them to the underside of a submerged rock, or the eggs may be retained in her body where only one or two of them survive, nourished by the other eggs. The mother gives birth to well-developed larvae.

Geographic distribution. The Karst regions of Italy and Yugoslavia: the Dalmation coast.

Habitat. Subterranean waters of limestone caves.

Population. Although not in grave danger of extinction, or even particularly scarce, the Olm is rare because of its extremely restricted range.

A F R I C A

INDRI
Indri Indri

CLASS
Mammals

SUBCLASS
Eutheria

ORDER
Primates

SUBORDER
Prosimiae

FAMILY
Indriidae

GENUS
Indri

Description. The Indri is the largest of the surviving lemurs, and measures 26 - 30in (66 -78 cm), including its short tail which varies from one to two inches (3 - 5 cm). It has a rounded head with a protruding bare muzzle and large yellow-brown eyes. It has thick silky fur which is longer on the shoulders and back. It is black on its back, hands, feet, upper parts of the limbs, and around the face. The rest of the body is light grey or slightly tawny. Colour does not vary in the sexes. Completely black (melanistic) or white individuals have been seen. Indris are diurnal and feed on leaves, flowers, and fruit. They search for food early in the morning and in the late afternoon. They are arboreal and agile tree-climbers, leaping from tree to tree, catching hold of the branches with their powerful hind feet. They climb trees by hugging the trunk with all four limbs and pushing up the lower part of their body. When jumping short distances they hold their body vertical; over longer leaps they project themselves horizontally. They spend much of their time resting on trees, clasping the trunk with all four limbs, or perching on forked branches. On the ground they move awkwardly, upright with slow steps or hopping. They live in small family groups consisting of between two and four animals. Little is known of the Indri in the wild because they are rarely seen. They have a shrill cry, often with various groups chattering to one another through the dense undergrowth. They are audible to humans for up to one mile (2 km). Very little is known about their reproductive habits. It is believed that a single offspring is born. The female chooses a quiet isolated spot to give birth. Much of the information about these creatures comes from local accounts: in tribal legends lemurs were thought to house the souls of ancestors.

Geographic distribution. Exclusive to Madagascar where they were once relatively widespread. They are now restricted to the north-eastern sector of the island.

Habitat. Humid rain forest.

Population. The now restricted area inhabited by the Indri, together with the extremely low density of the Indri population, indicate that the species is very rare and becoming endangered as its habitat shrinks. It was formerly protected by the local taboo traditions which are gradually disappearing. It is now fully protected by law, though this is more difficult to enforce in the remoter areas. Its habitat has been greatly devastated by deforestation and fires, and numbers have declined rapidly. The strict protection laws are now probably too late to guarantee the survival of this species. The Masoala and Betampona nature reserves are not very large. The Perinet-Analamazaotra Faunal Reserve was established mainly to protect the Indri, and it does have a number of individuals. However, in order for the Indri to survive its habitat must be preserved and the continuing deforestation curtailed. These animals are extremely rare in captivity.

BLACK LEMUR
Lemur macaco

CLASS
Mammals

SUBCLASS
Eutheria

ORDER
Primates

SUBORDER
Prosimiae

FAMILY
Lemuridae

GENUS
Lemur

Description. This is the smallest of the genus *Lemur*, measuring 3ft (92cm), including the 20-in (50-cm) tail. Colouring varies according to sex: males are black and females reddish brown. They live in groups of about ten – usually with a predominance of males – led by an adult female. Each group has its own territory which is marked out by odorous secretions. Unlike other lemur species which sleep in a sitting position, the Black Lemur sleeps on its belly on a branch, with its limbs hanging down. It is nocturnal and vegetarian. Mating takes place between May and July. After a four and a half-month gestation period a single offspring is born, occasionally two. They weigh 2 – 3oz (70 – 80g) and are suckled for six months. Young males reach maturity at 18 months. Black Lemurs are long-living; some individuals have lived up to 27 years in captivity.

Geographic distribution. Originally covered a vast area of Madagascar from the north-west coast to the Bay of Bombetoka in the south. Now it is restricted to a much smaller area in the Sambirona territory to the south of Ampasindava Bay, and on the islands of Nosy Bé and Nosy Komba.

Habitat. This arboreal mammal prefers humid forests. Much of its original habitat has been destroyed by agriculture – plantations of cocoa, cereals and ylang-ylang – and the spreading of human settlements. The Black Lemur has partially adapted to the new vegetation and often feeds on the crops. This has meant that the local population – who would not previously have harmed this species because of local taboo traditions – now uses every possible means to destroy them, although they are a protected species. There is a population of Black Lemurs on the Lokobe Reserve on Nosy Bé where the natural habitat has been preserved.

Population. It was once abundant because of the tolerance of the local population. Now numbers are falling drastically and the species is becoming endangered. In restricted areas it has adapted to the change in its environment and made use of it – feeding on fruit plantations – and they are still fairly numerous. These could be captured in order to repopulate other suitable territories and thereby ensure the species' survival. They are protected, but it is difficult to enforce these laws in the more remote areas. They are kept in many zoos, and there are self-sustaining populations. The closely related Brown Lemur, which is sometimes considered conspecific with the Black, is one of the more widespread species (it also occurs on the Comoro Islands, probably as a result of human introduction), but many populations are declining.

AYE-AYE
Daubentonia madagascariensis

CLASS
Mammals

SUBCLASS
Eutheria

ORDER
Primates

SUBORDER
Prosimiae

INFRAORDER
Lemuriformes

FAMILY
Daubentoniidae

GENUS
Daubentonia

Description. The Aye-aye is easily recognized by its bizarre appearance which distinguishes it from other lemur forms. It is the only living member of its family. It is 3ft (1m) in length; a good three fifths of this is the long, extremely hairy tail. Its murky, black colour show up the white colouring of the muzzle, cheeks, throat and two spots above the eye. The head is round, the auricles smooth, pendulous and membranous. The round eyes have a forward stare; the body is slight; the limbs are graceful, with long supple fingers. The incisors, long and crooked like a rodent's, are of similar structure and also grow continuously. The Aye-aye is arboreal and nocturnal. It is a solitary animal travelling alone over its own hunting ground of around 14 acres (6ha). It has only been sighted singly, though some authorities say the species lives in pairs. The food consists of fruit, bamboo shoots, sugar cane and, in particular, birds' eggs and insect larvae. The Aye-aye has a unique way of extracting the insects. It moves over the trunk or branch and then strikes the wood with its third digit (illustrated in the detail below). Next it listens to the noise caused by the movement of the insects inside. It then bites away the opening to the hole, puts in the third finger as a probe and, with its curved nail, hooks out the prey. Apart from catching insects, this middle finger is used to hit anything that attracts the animals' attention, to comb its coat, to remove parasites and as a means of scratching itself. The other fingers are meanwhile bent against the palm. The Aye-aye uses its fingers to scoop up water to drink. It always moves on four legs but can climb vertically. When it is on the ground, the tail is carried in the shape of an "S" as with other lemurs. It has a short strident cry, sounding like two pieces of metal grating together. During the day it rests in a hole in a tree or in a hollow between branches. According to some authorities, it makes a spherical nest of leaves. The female certainly builds a nest for protection when she gives birth, but little is known of the Aye-aye's sexual habits and reproductive cycle.

Geographic distribution. The first studies of this species indicated its presence in Madagascar's coastal forest and in all the low-altitude forests in the north, west and east of the island. Now, as far as it is possible to judge, there are only a few individuals scattered in the north-east and probably in the north-west coastal area.

Habitat. A forest-dweller, the Aye-aye depends on vegetation where the wood-eating insect, its principal food, can be found. Exploitation of the forest has created an anomalous situation to which the Aye-aye has responded with two slight adaptations: moving from the low-lying forest to the high forest, and occupying the old mango plantations created by the first colonizers. The species' drop in numbers shows, however, that these adaptations have not stopped its decline.

Population. A small reserve was set up at Mahambo where a few individual Aye-aye settled in 1957. Nine were introduced to the island of Nosy-Mangabé in 1967 where the conditions are favourable for them, and they are believed to be breeding there. The rarity of the Aye-aye, its infrequency of reproduction and our inadequate knowledge of the species make renewed efforts for its preservation imperative. Only rarely has it been held in captivity, but it has lived for up to 23 years.

CLASS
Mammals

SUBCLASS
Eutheria

ORDER
Primates

SUBORDER
Proscimiae

FAMILY
Indriidae

GENUS
Propithecus

VERREAUX'S SIFAKA
Propithecus verreauxi

Description. Verreaux's Sifaka is 3 – 4ft (1 – 1.5m) in length, half of which is the tail. The face is black and the rest of the body varies from white to light grey. It has long soft fur with a woolly undercoat. Sifakas are arboreal and move from branch to branch, often leaping 40ft (12m). Only rarely do they travel on the ground, hopping on their hind legs with their arms bent over their heads to help balance. They are diurnal creatures and spend most of the day sunning themselves on branches; during the hottest part they move into the shade. They live in groups of three to seven, occasionally up to nine. They gather food in groups calling to one another with their shrieking cry. They feed on leaves, flowers, bark and fruit. Mating takes place in February and March. After five month's gestation a single offspring is born. There are also various subspecies: P.v. majori inhabits an unprotected area and is the most threatened.

Geographic distribution. Limited to the western sector of Madagascar.

Habitat. Dense evergreen and deciduous forests with mixed vegetation.

Population. Figures for each subspecies vary, but taken as a whole the Sifaka population is fast becoming endangered. This is due to the continuing destruction of their natural habitat – aggravated by frequent forest fires. The local taboo systems which previously protected the Sifakas have also disappeared. Although it is protected, it is difficult to enforce in the remoter areas. The three reserves, Andohahela, Ankarafantiska, and Tsingy de Namoroka, together with two private reserves near Berenty and north of Mananara, offer some protection. The closely related Diademed Sifaka, Propithecus diadema, is also rare; its population had fallen to under 500 by the early 1970s.

PYGMY CHIMPANZEE
Pan paniscus

CLASS
Mammals

SUBCLASS
Eutheria

ORDER
Primates

SUBORDER
Simiae

FAMILY
Pongidae

GENUS
Pan

Description. In 1929 a new species of chimpanzee was recognized, set apart by its smaller, slimmer size and brownish black coat, and black face, called the Pygmy Chimpanzee. Its behaviour is very like that of the larger members of the species. As far as is known, the Pygmy Chimpanzee is social, living in groups of around 30; these are in a state of continual change because as some leave the group others will join it.

Geographic distribution. West central Africa, from the southern bank of the Zaire River to the southern end of the Kasi river and Sankuru.

Habitat. In practical terms the species adapts itself to prevailing conditions in the area: in the forest they are tree-living, but in the treeless savannah and scrubland with few plants they behave as if purely earthbound.

Population. There are no statistics on the population of the Pygmy Chimpanzee and the number in the wild has never been accurately recorded. As their habitat is increasingly occupied by man, the species' area is becoming very limited and it is easy to assume their numbers are dropping. The species is included in Class A of the African Convention, and therefore protected from hunting. Effective control is impossible in the most remote sectors and inevitably killing continues and the Pygmy Chimpanzee is not known to occur in any major national park or well-protected area. Only with a fuller knowledge of the species will it be possible to ensure valid protection. Only small numbers are kept in captivity, but it does breed regularly.

CLASS
Mammals

SUBCLASS
Eutheria

ORDER
Primates

SUBORDER
Simiae

FAMILY
Pongidae

GENUS
Gorilla

MOUNTAIN GORILLA
Gorilla gorilla beringei

Description. The Mountain Gorilla used to be considered a species by itself; but the characteristics on which this was based were hardly valid, and now it is thought by most authorities to be simply a well-defined subspecies. It has characteristics similar to the typical subspecies *Gorilla gorilla gorilla* (the Coastal Gorilla). The gorillas are the largest primates; on all fours, the male reaches a height of 5ft 9in (1.75m) - similar to, or even a little taller than, the average man. Standing erect, as it does very occasionally, the gorilla can be 6ft 6in (2m) tall. The female is always smaller. She also weighs substantially less, 160 – 310lb (70 – 140kg) as against the male's 300 – 610lb (135 – 275kg). In captivity and in cases of obesity, a gorilla can top the scales at 770lb (350kg). Extensive study of gorillas in the wild has produced a lot of detailed information about their behaviour. They live in pairs, in families or even in quite large groups of up to 30. Each community has its own territory but is not intolerant of other gorillas which stray into it. In the groups a third are males. Following a nine and a half month pregnancy, the female gives birth to a single offspring which seems extraordinarily small beside its parents. It is suckled for six months, sometimes for a year, although from two to three months onwards it is taught to eat solid foods. In the wild, gorillas are vegetarian, preferring leaves, bark and shoots. Most of their food is bitter and fibrous. At night, the gorilla builds a nest out of branches roughly woven together. Unlike the chimpanzee, it does not know how to use wood or other objects as tools. The usual lifespan of the species is 40 years, but a Coastal Gorilla in Philadelphia Zoo reached more than 46 years of age.

Geographic distribution. Rwanda, Uganda, Zaire. This vast area gives a false impression, however, as the Mountain Gorilla is only present on the volcanic peaks of the Virunga range, and the mas-sif of Mount Kahuzi; although these span a number of states, the relevant territory is comparatively small.

Habitat. Mountain rain forest up to a considerable height. In some areas (Kahuzi-Biega National Park in Zaire) Mountain Gorillas also live in secondary forests. The forests are mainly bamboo, *Hypericum*, *Hagenia* and giant senecio.

Population. In the early 1970s there was an estimated population of 1,000 in the wild; 200–250 in the Kahuzi-Biega National Park and 375–400 in the Mount Virunga zone. While the Kahuzi-Biega population has remained much the same, the Virunga count showed a drastic drop in numbers because of man's interference, and by the mid 1970s the estimate was down to 275. Obviously the animal is in great danger even though a large part of its territory was made into a national park. Man's exploitation of the species' habitat remains a problem. The herds of animals kept by the Watussi on the wooded pastures present direct competition. Poaching has caused buffalo and elephant to migrate to places where they consume the gorilla's food resources. In 1969 24,700 acres (10,000h) of the Parc des Volcans in Rwanda were given over to the cultivation of chrysanthemums, thus altering the botanical environment and bringing in a workfroce that was not compatible with the requirements of a nature reserve. The present Rwanda government is striving to make up for the errors of its predecessors. There are only four national parks and reserves that contain Mountain Gorillas: Virunga and Kahuzi-Biega (Zaire), Parc des Volcans (Rwanda) and the Gorilla Game Reserve (Uganda). The Mountain Gorilla Project developed in Rwanda in the 1970s and 80s has successfully used Mountain Gorilla conservation as a major tourist attraction. The Mountain Gorilla population is increasing, and is extremely well protected, as well as being a valuable source of foreign exchange in the Rwandan economy.

CLASS
Mammals

SUBCLASS
Eutheria

ORDER
Carnivora

SUBORDER
Fissipedia

FAMILY
Felidae

SUBFAMILY
Acinonychinae

GENUS
Acinonyx

CHEETAH
Acinonyx jubatus

Description. Cheetahs are similar in appearance to leopards, but smaller, slimmer and with long supple legs. Adult males measure 6 – 7½ft (2 – 2.30m) in length, including the 24 – 31-in (60 – 80-cm) tail. It has a shoulder height of up to 33in (90cm) and weighs up to 130lb (60kg). Like other cats, cheetahs have 30 teeth, but the canines are compressed like those of the Canidae. Their eyes are yellowish brown with round pupils. The supple paws have non-retractile claws. The coat varies from yellow to burnt ocher with paler underparts. The entire body is evenly covered with black spots. Oblique black stripes run down each side of the face from eye to mouth and the tip of the tail has dark bands. It has a very short dark mane from which it takes the name *jubatus*. The gestation period lasts 90 – 95 days. The female chooses a sheltered area in long grass or thicket to give birth. Between one and five cubs are born with a yellowish grey coat and lighter mane which extends from the top of the head down the back; and which they lose after ten weeks. The cubs weigh 10oz (280g) at birth. Cheetahs can attain speeds of up to 62 miles (100km) per hour over a distance of half a mile (500m). They avoid areas inhabited by man, but once captured they adapt easily to captivity and can be domesticated. The cheetah was used for hunting by the Ancient Egyptians and Sumerians. Marco Polo described the sight of a thousand cheetahs being taken out to hunt at the court of the Great Khan in the accounts of his travels. The Asiatic subspecies (*A. jubatus venaticus*) is similar to the African cheetah but slightly smaller. In Zimbabwe, one particular variety, the Royal, has a wonderful coat on which the spots on the flanks and back fuse to form almost longitudinal stripes. It is not considered a separate subspecies in its own right and is a sort of "tabby" cheetah.

Geographic distribution. The cheetah once inhabited Asia from India to the Red Sea and extended across the whole of the African continent except for the humid tropical forests and the central band of the Sahara Desert. It still exists in a large part of its original range in Africa but in substantially diminshed numbers, except where it is protected in parks and reserves. The Asiatic subspecies is almost extinct throughout its original territory and may still occur in the arid zone on the borders of Afghanistan and Turkmenistan and in some parts of eastern Iran.

Habitat. Found mainly in arid savannah and occasionally in high grassland and on the edges of forests. The Asiatic subspecies appears to be adapted to even drier regions. Agriculture and spreading human populations have reduced and destroyed much of its habitat.

Population. The position of the African cheetah is extremely vulnerable; extinct in many areas and greatly reduced in others. The Asiatic cheetah has also disappeared from a large part of its original territory and is considered in grave danger of extinction. However, it seems to be increasing in Iran where there are 200 – 300 examples. None have been sighted in India since 1951. The African population probably totals less than 25,000 (there were probably only 100,000 even a century ago). It is still reasonably widespread and abundant only in Namibia, and protected in almost all of Africa.

LEOPARD
Panthera pardus

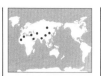

Description. The leopard is the most widespread cat of the genus *Panthera*. There are several subspecies distributed throughout a very wide range across Africa and Asia. Sizes vary considerably amongst the various subspecies and males are generally larger than females. Adult males can measure 5 – 8ft (1.5 – 2.5m) in length; one third of this is the tail. It has a streamlined body with proportionately short legs. It carries its long tail curved upwards, giving this cat an elegance not often encountered in other carnivores. Its distinct coat varies from yellow-grey to deep yellow (again depending on the different subspecies). The rosettes are dark, almost black, and cover the entire body. Black leopards (melanistic) – Black Panthers – are relatively common. Throughout Africa and Asia the stealth and beauty of this creature have earned it almost supernatural qualities amongst local populations. It is a solitary hunter and usually stays within a well-defined territory provided there is sufficient prey. It is not certain whether the female also has her own marked territory. Principally nocturnal, the leopard hunts from sunset through the night. It ambushes prey by waiting in trees, in hollows, or kills them after a long chase. If the prey is too large to be consumed in one night it will often haul the carcass up a tree, away from the reach of marauding hyenas or jackals. Its strength is prodigious considering it is no bigger than a large dog. African leopards eat monkeys, mandrills, gnu and other large herbivores. If these are scarce it will eat smaller animals such as rodents, birds and fish. Asian leopards hunt monkeys, deer, buffalo, ibex, wild boar and smaller mammals. Leopards mate for life but males and females only hunt together during the mating season. The gestation period lasts 100 days; between two and four (occasionally one and five) cubs are born. Leopards reach sexual maturity at around three years in the wild.

Habitat. Leopards occur in a wide variety of habitats and are amongst the most adaptable of mammals. Their habitat includes tropical forest, dense jungle, arid savannah and rocky mountainous zones.

Geographic distribution. Africa and most of southern Asia from Turkey to China; Sri Lanka; Java (where examples of Black Panthers are fairly common).

Population. The current population is not known as it is spread over such a vast area. Many of the subspecies are restricted to specific areas where the habitat is gradually being destroyed. Hunting has been the prime cause for the rapid decline in numbers; its fur has always been highly prized. It is now protected in most of its range, but obviously difficult to enforce in the more remote areas. The subspecies most in danger are: the Barbary Leopard (*P.p.panthera*) from Morocco, Algeria, and Tunisia, probably numbering no more than a few dozen; the South Arabian Leopard (*P.p.nimr*) from the mountainous regions of the southern tip of the Arabian peninsula; the Anatolian Leopard (*P.p.tulliana*) from Turkey; the Amur Leopard (*P.p.orientalis*); from eastern Siberia and northern Korea; the Sinai Leopard (*P.p.jarvisi*) from Sinai. They are common in zoos and reproduce fairly easily in captivity.

BROWN HYENA
Hyaena brunnea

CLASS
Mammals

SUBCLASS
Eutheria

ORDER
Carnivora

SUBORDER
Fissipedia

FAMILY
Hyaenidae

GENUS
Hyaena

Description. The two most common and best known species are the Spotted Hyena (*Crocuta crocuta*) which once inhabited almost the whole of Africa as far north as the Sahara, and the Striped Hyena (*Hyaena hyaena*) of northern, central and eastern Africa and south-west Asia. Closely related to the latter is the rare and less well known Brown Hyena (*Hyaena brunnea*) of southern Africa. Similar to the Striped Hyena in appearance (and size) but has longer hair (up to 10in [25cm] long) which is greyish coloured on the head and uniformly brown over the body. The dorsal mane is pale grey. It usually hangs down partially covering the body, but can also stand on end. Its legs have light chestnut stripes. It has a massive head, large ears and powerful jaws. The Brown Hyena is the most timid of its species: it is active only at night. It feeds on small prey, such as hares, eggs and insects. The female gives birth to between two and six young (normally three to four) after a gestation period of about three months.

Geographic distribution. Formerly throughout southern Africa as far north as Zimbabwe, Mozambique and Angola.

Habitat. Low, arid, savannah regions with sparse tree and bush growth; open plains and thinly forested areas. In general, the Brown Hyena never occupies the same territory as the Spotted Hyena which prefers a less arid habitat.

Population. Brown hyenas are still relatively abundant in the Kalahari and Gemsbok National Park (Botswana and Namibia). They are regularly bred in zoos.

MOUNTAIN ZEBRA
Equus zebra

CLASS
Mammals

SUBCLASS
Eutheria

ORDER
Perissodactyla

SUBORDER
Hippomorpha

FAMILY
Equidae

GENUS
Equus

Description. This species is characterized by the grid-shaped markings on the rump; the body is covered with closely-spaced parallel stripes. The Mountain Zebra is up to 4ft 3in (1.30m) tall. There are two subspecies: the Cape Mountain Zebra which is slightly smaller and Hartmann's Zebra (illustrated right) which is a little larger and has thinner stripes.

Geographic distribution. The Cape Mountain Zebra inhabits only two reserves in the mountains in southern Cape Province; Hartmann's Zebra inhabits the mountainous part of south-west Africa (Namibia) and southern Angola.

Habitat. Rugged mountain areas.

Population. The Cape Zebra was reduced to only 47 examples in 1937 which were transferred to a reserve. Its number has now increased to over 200. Hartmann's Zebra numbers about 15,000.

GIANT ELAND
Taurotragus derbianus derbianus

CLASS
Mammals

SUBCLASS
Eutheria

ORDER
Artiodactyla

SUBORDER
Ruminantia

FAMILY
Bovidae

SUBFAMILY
Tragelaphinae

GENUS
Taurotragus

Description. The Giant Eland can measure 14ft (3.50m) in length, including tail, and stand 6ft (1.80m) tall. The long horns are spirally twisted and grow close together. It has a dewlap which it frequently drags along the ground through mud and even urine and then rubs on to the branches of trees or shrubs to mark out its territory.

Geographic distribution. Very limited numbers throughout an area from Senegal to the Ivory Coast, covering Gambia, Mali, and Guinea, east to south-west Sudan and north-west Uganda.

Habitat. Shrub-covered or preferably tree-covered savannah.

Population. Exact population unknown. It is fully protected in the national park of Niokolo-Kobo in Senegal and Garamba National Park, Zaire; theoretically it is protected throughout its range.

CLASS
Mammals

SUBCLASS
Eutheria

ORDER
Perissodactyla

SUBORDER
Hippomorpha

FAMILY
Equidae

GENUS
Equus

AFRICAN WILD ASS

Equus asinus

Description. Three subspecies of African Wild Ass once roamed the desert and semi-arid areas of northern Africa: the Nubian Wild Ass (*Equus asinus africanus*, illustrated opposite, above left), the North African Wild Ass (*Equus asinus atlanticus*), and the Somalian Wild Ass (*Equus asinus somalicus*, illustrated opposite, center). The North African Wild Ass has been extinct for some time. African Wild Asses are medium-sized with a shoulder height of 3½ − 4½ft (1.10 − 1.40m). The Nubian Wild Ass is slightly smaller in stature. They are well-proportioned, elegant animals with long slim legs and graceful pointed ears. They have short manes and the colour of their coat varies from pure grey to yellowish or reddish grey. Nubian Wild Asses have a dark thin stripe running down their back and intersected by a latitudinal stripe across the shoulders — like a cross. The Somalian Wild Ass has only the dark stripe running down its back (not always present), and its limbs are ringed by dark bands. African Wild Asses are gregarious. Before they became rare, large herds roamed the arid plains constantly in search of vegetation. They were usually led by a stallion or older female. They would never stray far from their territory and would feed on dry shrubs and any other vegetation available in the dry habitat of their range. They have extremely sharp hearing which ensures their safety in the vast open areas where they are susceptible to hungry predators. At the slightest sound of danger the leader will round the herd up and swiftly lead them to safety. They are in most danger when drought forces them to waterholes. There they are the easy prey of the big cats and man who hunts them both for their meat and skin. African Wild Asses can go for very long periods without water so fortunately it does not need to quench its thirst often. They are considered to be the ancestors of the domestic strain.

Geographic distribution. The North African Wild Ass was once widely distributed throughout northern Africa. Recent distribution of the Nubian Wild Ass occurred in the hill region around the Red Sea as far south as Ethiopia, but it is probably extinct now. The Somalian Wild Ass is found in Somalia and Ethiopia. The most numerous population is believed to be in western Ethiopia.

Habitat. Semi-desert areas with sparse vegetation and very little water.

Population. The African Wild Ass probably numbers less than 3,000 in the wild, but since the early 1970s it has been difficult to carry out surveys in the area. There is also a small captive population. It is protected throughout its range, though enforcement of protection is nearly impossible, particularly in Ethiopia where much of its current range is affected by warfare and severe drought.

BLACK RHINOCEROS
Diceros bicornis

CLASS
Mammals

SUBCLASS
Eutheria

ORDER
Perrisodactyla

SUBORDER
Ceratomorpha

FAMILY
Rhinocerotidae

GENUS
Diceros

Description. The Black Rhinoceros can grow to a length of 12ft (3.75m), excluding tail, with a shoulder height of 5ft (1.60m). It weighs about 3 tons. It feeds mainly on shoots and leaves which it tears away using its developed upper lip.

Geographic distribution. Once distributed in large numbers in Africa from Cape Province to southern Angola in the west and to Ethiopia in the east.

Habitat. Savannah with trees or bushes; open areas in forests, and grassland up to 10,000ft (3,000m).

Population. During the 1970s and 1980s there was a catastrophic decline due to poaching, probably as a result of widespread publicity concerning the high value of their horns. By the late 1970s less than 30,000 remained, and by 1984 these had fallen to 9,000 and continued to decline, with several populations becoming extinct. They are, however, bred regularly in zoos.

WHITE OR SQUARE-LIPPED RHINOCEROS
Ceratotherium simum cottoni

CLASS
Mammals

SUBCLASS
Eutheria

ORDER
Perrisodactyla

SUBORDER
Ceratomorpha

FAMILY
Rhinocerotidae

GENUS
Ceratotherium

Description. The White or Square-lipped Rhinoceros can be divided into two sub-species: the northern *Ceratotherium simum cottoni*, and the southern, and more common, *Ceratotherium simum simum*. There are few physical differences. The White Rhinoceros is the largest of all rhinoceroses, measuring up to 13ft (4m) in length, excluding tail, with a shoulder height of 6½ft (2m). It weighs at least 3 tons. It is distinguished by its square lip (unlike the Black Rhinoceros) which is suited for browsing.

Geographic distribution. The northern subspecies was once widespread in Africa between latitudes 13° and 9° North.

Habitat. Savannah and arid forests.

Population. Since the late 1980s less than 20 survive, all in the Garamba National Park, Zaire.

PYGMY HIPPOPOTAMUS
Choeropsis liberiensis

CLASS
Mammals

SUBCLASS
Eutheria

ORDER
Artiodactyla

SUBORDER
Nonruminantia

FAMILY
Hippopotamidae

GENUS
Choeropsis

Description. This species looks similar to a young Hippopotamus. It measures up to 5½ft (1.75m) in length and about 31in (80cm) tall. It weighs 400 − 575lb (180 − 260kg). The head is smaller and more rounded than that of the Hippopotamus. The mouth is very large; there is only one pair of lower incisors and the canines are developed into tusks. The skin is a blackish brown, sleek, hairless and kept constantly moist and oiled by the secretion of mucus. After a gestation period of about 100 days, the female gives birth to one young, weighing 9 − 13lb (4 − 6kg). The Pygmy Hippopotamus lives for 35 to 40 years. Very little is known of the habits of this species. It is possible to travel for days within its area of distribution without sighting one of them. It is nocturnal. They are very shy and will flee from the presence of man. It was thought that, unlike the common Hippopotamus which hides in water, the Pygmy Hippopotamus would take to the forest when threatened. However, it is now believed that they have a network of paths, rather like tunnels, that lead directly to nearby river or swamps, which they use when in danger. The species feeds off water plants, leaves, algae, grasses and fruit.

Geographic distribution. The swampy forests of West Africa − Sierra Leone, Guinea, Liberia and the Ivory Coast.

Habitat. The Pygmy Hippopotamus is less aquatic than the common Hippopotamus. It inhabits inaccessible tropical forest and thick vegetation on river banks.

Population. The species is very rare. Its decline has been caused by the destruction of its habitat and by intensive hunting for its meat. It has been protected since the African Convention of 1969. The species adapts very well to captivity and reproduces well in zoos.

ARABIAN ORYX

Oryx leucoryx

Description. The Arabian Oryx is the smallest and rarest of the four species of antelope belonging to the genus *Oryx*. It has a shoulder height of about 3ft (1m); other species grow up to 5ft (1.50m). It weighs about 220lbs (100Kg). The coat is almost pure white except for the blackish brown legs; darker at the front than the back, with white pasterns; the hooves are broader and more rounded than those of other species. It is slightly humped. There are black patches on the forehead, nose, and cheeks. The tail is white with a thick black tuft. Some examples have a faint dark stripe on the flank. The thin horns can measure up to 2½ft (75cm) in length and are very pointed; they grow almost straight, curving only slightly backwards, and ringed. They are a formidable weapon: when attacked, the Arabian Oryx will lower its head with the horns pointing directly forward. In this way it scares off even the largest predators. One young is born after a gestation period of about 260 days. The species lives up to 20 years.

Geographic distribution. The Arabian Oryx was once distributed over almost the entire Arabian peninsula; from Mesopotamia to Sinai and perhaps as far north as Syria. It became extinct in the wild in the 1960s or 1970s.

Habitat. Rocky or sandy desert areas where it finds the vegetation on which it feeds. It can go for long periods without water and cover great distances in search of pasture. It uses its hooves and horns to dig hollows beneath shrubs or in sand dunes to hide or shelter from the sun.

Population. This species became extinct in the wild but was preserved in captivity. Its decline was brought about by excessive hunting, especially during recent decades as the wealth of the local populations increased due to the exploitation of oil. The Oryx was killed through organized hunting when the herds were followed by jeeps and other forms of motor vehicle and shot with automatic weapons and sub-machine guns. However, in 1962 the Fauna Preservation Society of London launched "Operation Oryx" in order to save the species. Its aim was to capture a sufficient number to form a nucleus from which to breed the species in captivity and then reintroduce it to its native habitat. Three animals were captured, another was donated by London Zoo, one was donated by the Sultanate of Kuwait, and four were given to the World Wide Fund for Nature by the King of Saudi Arabia. This nucleus of nine animals was then called the World Herd and was placed in Phoenix Zoo, Arizona, which has a similar climate to Arabia. The animals have reproduced with success and their number has risen annually. In 1972, in order to avoid the risk of disease, some were transferred to the wild animal park at San Diego, California. In 1979 the World Herd had 68 Arabian Oryx, 43 at Phoenix and 25 at San Diego, California. By the mid 1980s the species could be considered safe, with several captive herds in different locations (an insurance against disease wiping them out), and those reintroduced into Oman breeding and spreading back over their former range. There were over 1,000 in captivity by the end of the 1980s.

SCIMITAR-HORNED ORYX

Oryx tao – Oryx dammah

CLASS
Mammals

SUBCLASS
Eutheria

ORDER
Artiodactyla

SUBORDER
Ruminantia

FAMILY
Bovidae

SUBFAMILY
Hippotraginae

GENUS
Oryx

Description. This species is similar in looks to the more common Gazelle Oryx but has very long horns which curve distinctly backwards. Adult males reach over 4ft (1.25m) at the shoulders and weigh over 440lb (200kg). The coat is off-white with brown shading on the muzzle, neck, flanks, and upperparts of the legs. A desert animal, it can survive for months without water.

Geographic distribution. Once inhabited almost all Sahel to the north and south of the Sahara, from West Africa to the Red Sea.

Habitat. Semi-desert edges of the Sahara.

Population. By the 1980s they were virtually extinct in the wild. However, there were substantial captive herds and as a result of an initiative similar to that for the Arabian Oryx, captive stocks were made available for reintroduction in the wild.

ADDAX

Addax nasomaculatus

CLASS
Mammals

SUBCLASS
Eutheria

ORDER
Artiodactyla

SUBORDER
Ruminantia

FAMILY
Bovidae

SUBFAMILY
Hippotraginae

GENUS
Addax

Description. The Addax is similar to the Oryx. Its length, excluding tail, is just under 6½ft (2m) and it stands 4ft (1.20m) at the shoulders. It weighs up to 275lb (125kg). The Ancient Egyptians reared them as beasts of burden and as sacrificial victims.

Geographic distribution. At one time the Addax was distributed throughout the Sahara Desert.

Habitat. Desert areas with sand dunes.

Population. No more than several dozen in Algeria, Niger and the Sudan. In 1960 5,636 were recorded in Mauritania-Mali at Majabat-al-Kubra; 1,500 lived in northern Chad in 1970. By the 1980s its status in the wild and in captivity was very similar to its compatriot, the Scimitar-horned Oryx.

WHITE-TAILED GNU

Connochaetes gnou

CLASS
Mammals

SUBCLASS
Eutheria

ORDER
Artiodactyla

SUBORDER
Ruminantia

FAMILY
Bovidae

SUBFAMILY
Alcelaphinae

GENUS
Connochaetes

Description. The Gnu is undoubtedly the strangest looking of all the antelopes. Its body is similar to a horse's; high at the shoulders and dipping down at the back. The tail is also long like a horse's, with a white tip. The Gnu has an ox-like head and both sexes have curved horns (smaller in the female). These grow downwards from the top of the head towards the eyes and then curve sharply upwards. The hair also grows strangely; tufts of longer hair grow around the eyes and chin, and between the front legs. A mane extends down the neck to shoulders. An adult male can measure 6½ft (2m) in length, excluding tail, and stand 4ft (1.20m) tall, weighing 400lb (180kg). The coat is chocolate brown. Very little has been written about the White-tailed Gnu which was virtually brought to the brink of extinction by the beginning of the century. It is thought, however, to have similar habits to other antelopes which are numerous in the African savannah. The Gnu is gregarious and would once have lived in the wild in large herds of about 50, together with other antelopes, zebras, and ostriches. Although it is usually very calm and tranquil, the animal will suddenly and for no apparent reason, leap into the air, race around and show off. It will stop just as suddenly and resume its placid browsing.

Geographic distribution. Once inhabited a large part of South Africa: Karoo Cape Province, southern Transvaal, and Natal. Today it is only found in zoos, parks and private reserves.

Habitat. Grassland and semi-desert scrubland.

Population. The species was saved thanks to private intervention. In 1965 the entire population of 1,700 – 1,800 was found on private ranches. By 1970 there were over 3,000 and reintroduction into reserves subsequently took place.

SLENDER-HORNED GAZELLE
Gazella leptoceros

Description. The Slender-horned Gazelle is one of the rarest species of the genus *Gazella*. It is a medium-sized gazelle with a shoulder height of 28in (72cm) and weighs about 68lb (28kg), and is easily distinguished by its pale sand-coloured, almost white, coat. The tail is darker with a blackish tip. Its horns are long, slim, and almost vertical. The hooves are long and slender – slightly splayed to facilitate moving over sandy areas. Generally a single offspring is born which is able to follow its mother after a few days. Within two weeks it is nearly as swift as its parents. It can live up to 12 years.

Geographic distribution. Once inhabited all the desert regions of North Africa. Now it is restricted to the very northern part of its original range: the desert regions of Algeria, Tunisia, Libya, Egypt, the Sudan and Chad.

Habitat. A truly desert-living animal which prefers to inhabit sand dunes where few other mammals manage to survive. During periods of severe drought it leaves the dunes in search of food elsewhere. It eats desert vegetation and has very little need of water.

Population. The species was once numerous wherever the desert provided sufficient vegetation to support it. Numbers have been reduced drastically due to intensive hunting and the destruction of its habitat. It has been virtually impossible to estimate numbers because of the inaccessibility of its habitat. Although protected by the African Convention of 1969, stricter protection measures and the creation of reserves within its range are required to ensure its survival. There are small numbers in captivity, the largest group is in San Diego Wild Animal Park, U.S.A.

ABYSSINIAN IBEX
Capra walie

CLASS
Mammals

SUBCLASS
Eutheria

ORDER
Artiodactyla

SUBORDER
Ruminantia

FAMILY
Bovidae

SUBFAMILY
Caprinae

GENUS
Capra

Description. The two species in grave danger of extinction are the Abyssinian Ibex (*Capra walie*) and the Pyrenean Ibex (*Capra pyrenaica*). The Abyssinian Ibex is similar to the Ibex (*Capra ibex*). It stands 3ft (1m) at shoulder height and the adult male has horns 3½ft (1.15m) long, with a boney protruberance on the forehead. The coat is brown, redder on the upper parts of the body and paler underneath; the female is lighter in colour and smaller in size with slender, slightly arched horns measuring about 12in (30cm). One or occasionally two young are born between May and June after a gestation period of 150-180 days. The Pyrenean Ibex is distinguished by horns that curve backwards and outwards. Males live in separate groups only joining the females for the mating season in December and January. The Ibex lives for up to 15 years but can live for over 20 years in captivity.

Geographic distribution. The Abyssinian Ibex lives exclusively on the Simien Mountains (14,800ft [4,500m]) in Ethiopia. It is probable that it has never lived outside this area. Until a few centuries ago the Pyrenean Ibex lived on both sides of the Pyrenees, but is now limited to the extreme north of the Huesca province in Spain.

Habitat. Mountainous: high peaks in summer and the lower slopes in autumn and winter.

Population. The decline of the Abyssinian Ibex is primarily due to the destruction of its habitat; hunting has also played a considerable part. In the 1970s there were about 300, of which 240 were in the Simien Mountains National Park, Ethiopia. However, there is little recent news. The Pyrenean Ibex is considered in grave danger of extinction.

CLASS
Aves

SUBCLASS
Neornithes

ORDER
Falconiformes

FAMILY
Falconidae

SUBFAMILY
Falconinae

GENUS
Falco

MAURITIUS KESTREL
Falco punctatus

Description. One of the rarest birds in the world, at one time it seemed that its extinction was very close. The species is closely related to the African Kestrel (*Falco rupicoloides*) and the Madagascar Kestrel (*Falco newtoni*), although these are larger. The Mauritius Kestrel measures 10in (23 - 25cm) long. The plumage is similar to the female Old World Kestrel (*Falco tinnunculus*); although it does not have the dark stripes like moustaches to the side of the beak. The upper parts of the body are a red-brown colour with small black spots, and the underparts are whitish with brown or black spots. The tail has a dark band at its tip. The eyes are black and surrounded by a circle of bare yellow skin. The legs are yellow with black claws. The female lays three or four eggs which are incubated for about 30 days; the young are then reared by both parents. The species feeds on lizards and ground prey.

Geographic distribution. It is believed that this species has always been limited to the island of Mauritius in the Indian Ocean.

Habitat. The forests of Mauritius.

Population. A century ago the Mauritius Kestrel was common throughout the island and even 50 years ago it was fairly common. By 1974 it is believed only six birds remained in the wild, but by 1984 there were six pairs in the wild and ten birds in captivity. In the following few years both wild and captive populations grew rapidly, and 21 birds were released in 1988.

CLASS
Aves

SUBCLASS
Neornithes

ORDER
Ciconiiformes

FAMILY
Threskiornithidae

SUBFAMILY
Threskiornithinae

GENUS
Geronticus

NORTHERN BALD IBIS
Geronticus eremita

Description. Known also by the Bavarian name Waldrapp (Wood Crow), this bird was once widespread in Germany, Austria and Switzerland. It was one of the first creatures to become protected. In 1504 Archbishop Leonard of Salzburg decreed it a protected species. The nestlings had long been a delicacy on the tables of the rich. Although the decree was renewed annually, it was virtually ignored, and the Northern Bald Ibis disappeared from Europe and was forgotten in the space of a century. When a large colony was discovered in Syria in 1854, it was treated as a new species and was only connected with the Northern Bald Ibis in 1906. It has a long, downward-curving, red beak and a bare reddish head with grey cap. Long dark feathers around the neck form a tuft and ruff. The long strong legs are red. Three or four eggs are laid at the beginning of April and incubated for about 28 days. The young are able to fly by early June. It feeds on insects, larvae, and small reptiles and amphibians.

Geographic distribution. Until the seventeenth century it was distributed in Europe. Today it survives only in parts of Morocco and in the Turkish city of Birecik on the Euphrates.

Habitat. Rocky overhangs and cracks in steep cliffs.

Population. In 1976 there were only 39 birds. Despite protection and other conservation measures, in 1986 they still numbered only 35. By the late 1980s there were around 500 in numerous zoos, probably all bred in captivity.

CLASS
Aves

SUBCLASS
Neornithes

ORDER
Passeriformes

FAMILY
Muscicapidae

SUBFAMILY
Monarchinae

GENUS
Terpsiphone

SEYCHELLES BLACK PARADISE-FLYCATCHER

Terpsiphone corvina

Description. The genus *Terpsiphone* includes various species of flycatcher which have brilliant colours, very long tails, and are known as "Paradise Flycatchers." Among the most beautiful of these is the Seychelles Black Paradise-flycatcher. It is also the rarest. The male is a splendid black colour with shades of midnight blue; it is 18in (46cm) long, including the slender 12-in (30-cm) central tail feathers. The female (illustrated below left) is brown with yellow-white underparts and a black head. They eat insects which they catch among leaves and shrubs. The nests are built high on very slender branches that will not support the weight of such predators as cats, snakes, and rats. The nest is a deep but tiny bowl into which two or three eggs are laid. The incubation period lasts about 12 days.

Geographic distribution. Originally found over the entire Seychelles archipelago. Today it survives only on the island of La Digue.

Habitat. High, tree-covered areas of the Seychelles.

Population. The species was fairly numerous up to 1960, but is now estimated at around 60, but fluctuating.

SEYCHELLES OWL
Otus insularis

CLASS
Aves

SUBCLASS
Neornithes

ORDER
Strigiformes

FAMILY
Strigidae

SUBFAMILY
Buboninae

GENUS
Otus

Description. The Seychelles Owl is 10in (25cm) long with wings reaching up to 11in (28cm): the tarsi are featherless. Like all owls, it is basically active at dusk, and eats insects and occasionally small reptiles.
Geographic distribution. Mahé Island, although probably at one time it also inhabited the other islands of the Seychelles archipelago.
Habitat. Moss-covered forest to a height of 3,280ft (1,000m).
Population. In 1906 the species was considered extinct. In 1959, however, a small group was discovered in one of the mountain areas of Mahé where they were nesting. The species has declined as a result of the competition from other species, such as barn owls, and the destruction of its habitat.

SEYCHELLES KESTREL
Falco ararea

CLASS
Aves

SUBCLASS
Neornithes

ORDER
Falconiformes

FAMILY
Falconidae

SUBFAMILY
Falconinae

GENUS
Falco

Description. The Seychelles Kestrel is 7in (18cm) long, with brown plumage on the upper parts of the body, black-flecked on the shoulder feathers, with bluish-grey and black wing feathers. Females usually lay two eggs. It feeds off lizards.
Geographic distribution. Up to 1940 the species was distributed over the entire Seychelles archipelago; it is now only found on Mahé.
Habitat. The coral sand dunes of this island.
Population. The reason for the species' decline is unknown, although it is probably due to the introduction of barn owls. Its population is also unknown, although it is very small and diminishing.

ASIA

WOLF
Canis lupus

CLASS
Mammals

SUBCLASS
Eutheria

ORDER
Carnivora

SUBORDER
Fissipedia

FAMILY
Canidae

SUBFAMILY
Caninae

GENUS
Canis

Description. The wolf looks like the German Shepherd Dog (Alsatian) and its size varies considerably. Some authorities divide the wolf into subspecies according to geographic distribution. The male can grow up to 34in (85cm) in height and 5½ft (1.70m) in length, including the tail. It weighs 175lb (80kg). It has a lithe body with a broad chest; the tail is usually carried low. The teeth, unlike those of most other Canidae, are extremely powerful; it is said they can shatter the femur of an elk in one bite. The colour varies (there are dark, almost black wolves found in the south, and grey, almost white ones in the north). The coat is fairly short but in cold regions it is thicker with a ruff around the neck with very thick fur on the belly and haunches. The wolf is generally gregarious and lives off prey which it hunts in packs. As it always takes as prey the oldest, most sick and debilitated, it can be argued that the wolf carries out a form of natural selection. It seems from various studies that its social organization is similar to man's. According to W. Herre the fact that the wolf is able to feed off a wide range of animals shows that its organization is one of the most highly evolved amongst mammals. The prey, in fact, consists of medium to large animals, roe-deer or elk, depending on the area of distribution. In order to pursue and kill their prey collectively, the indivual wolves divide the work. Hunting is very hierarchical; the leader of the pack is usually an adult male. His main function is to maintain order and to make sure that the individuals respect their allotted tasks. He may not necessarily lead the pack in a physical sense: this task may be delegated to another, even a female. The mating season is between February and April. The hierarchy is also respected with regard to mating; it is very difficult for a lower-ranking male wolf to find a mate if there are others of a higher rank around. The gestation period is nine weeks, at the end of which the female gives birth to between three and ten pups, blind, helpless and unable to move.

The birth takes place in a sheltered, secure lair perhaps adapted by the female from a fox's or beaver's abandoned lair. After the first eight weeks of milk-feeding, rearing is also undertaken by the father and even by other young, usually female members of the pack. The young reach full size after one year and sexual maturity after three years. The wolf can live for up to ten years in the wild, but in captivity, like domestic dogs, they can live longer. They are successfully bred in captivity.

Geographic distribution. The distribution of the wolf still covers a large part of North America, a few European countries (it is extinct in the British Isles, Holland, Belgium, Denmark, France, Germany, Switzerland, Austria and Hungary), and Asia.

Habitat. The wolf lives in many different habitats and at different altitudes. It can be found in tundra, bush, evergreen or deciduous forest, open country or near towns in cultivated inhabited areas.

Population. The wolf has been reduced in numbers everywhere. It is, however, still quite common in Alaska, Canada and parts of Russia and Asia. The numbers vary according to the subspecies or species. Small numbers survive in Italy, Spain and Eastern Europe, and occasionally they cross from Russia into Scandinavia. The principal reason for the wolf's disappearance is the relentless hunting by man with traps, guns, snares and poison. The disappearance of game – again destroyed by man – which was part of the wolf's diet, has also aided its decline. Today the wolf is rigidly protected in many countries; a number also live in national parks and zoos.

GIANT PANDA
Ailuropoda melanoleuca

CLASS
Mammals

SUBCLASS
Eutheria

ORDER
Carnivora

SUBORDER
Fissipedia

FAMILY
Procyonidae

SUBFAMILY
Ailurinae

GENUS
Ailuropoda

Description. The Giant Panda has been the object of more affection and publicity than any other wild animal despite the fact that it was unknown in the Western World until 1869. (It has been known in China for at least 4,000 years and is mentioned in ancient documents.) In 1869, the French Jesuit naturalist, Father Armand David, described the animal for the first time, having studied the skins of two Pandas killed by Chinese hunters on Mup-ing Mountain. 47 years were to pass before another European, J.H. Edgar, a missionary, found an animal which he identified as the Panda asleep in an oak tree in the upper Yangtze valley. The attraction of the Giant Panda lies in its peculiar black and white markings, and the body shaped like a large bear cub's which make it look like a large teddy bear. In addition, its habit of sitting or lying on its back while tearing at the food it holds in its front paws makes its appeal irresistible – hence the popularity all over the world of thousands of different types of toy panda. The Chinese call the Giant Panda bei-shung, which means "white bear." An adult Panda grows to a length of 6ft (1.80m) and to a shoulder height of 30in (75cm); it weighs up to 300lb (135kg). Some consider that they belong to a family of their own, the Ailuropodidae, while most classify it with bears, a few with raccoons. The Giant Panda is a plantigrade, that is, it walks on the soles of its feet like bears. It is a very agile tree-climber. It does not hibernate in winter and is well adapted to the very low temperatures of its habitat. An essentially solitary creature, it makes its lair in cavities beneath protruding rocks or in hollow tree trunks, where it constructs a bed of bamboo. It spends almost its entire life roaming around the dense bamboo forest. Equipped with powerful jaws and broad, cuspidate molar teeth typical of carnivores, the Panda mainly eats fibrous bamboo shoots, although occasionally it hunts small mammals, birds and fish. The female normally gives birth to a single cub – rarely two – after a gestation period of about five months. At birth the cub weighs less that 11lb (450g) but it grows rapidly, reaching 66 to 77lb (30 to 35kg) at the end of the first year. The Panda may live for up to 15 years. An interesting characteristic is the highly flexible, small fleshy pads under each forepaw which the Giant Panda uses like thumbs to grasp slender bamboo shoots and hold them tight while it tears the leaves off with its mouth. The first Giant Panda to reach the West alive was Su-lin, a female cub captured by an American in 1936, and purchased by the Brookfield Zoo, Chicago.

Geographic distribution. Although in prehistoric times the Giant Panda was widely distributed over southern China, today it is found only in northern and central Szechwan, eastern Sinkiang, and in the east Tibetan plateau.

Habitat. Inhabits bamboo, coniferous and deciduous forest at altitudes of between 8,00 and 13,000ft (roughly 2,500 and 4,000m) in a cold humid climate. In summer it moves to higher mountain slopes.

Population. It has been strictly protected under Chinese law since 1939, and the the restricted zones in which it lives have been proclaimed nature reserves. The few that are found outside China today were mostly given by the government to important visitors or as pledges of peace to friendly countries. Only a few have been bred in zoos, mostly in China, and there are no self-sustaining captive populations. The capture of Pandas for zoos is probably one of the major threats to the populations currently. As they are used as political gifts it is difficult to prevent this trade. The Giant Panda is the symbol of the WWF.

CLOUDED LEOPARD
Neofelis nebulosa

CLASS
Mammals

SUBCLASS
Eutheria

ORDER
Carnivora

SUBORDER
Fissipedia

FAMILY
Felidae

SUBFAMILY
Felinae

GENUS
Neofelis

Description. The Clouded Leopard is a slender, agile, tree-climbing cat. Smaller than most other leopards, it reaches an overall length of up to 6½ft (2m), including a 3-ft (1-m) tail, and weighs up to 50lb (23kg). It has a large head with very long canine teeth, and broad spatulate paws. Its coat varies from dark grey or brown, to tawny yellow with white underparts. It is marked with large dark spots surrounded by lighter shades that give the coat a clouded effect. This arboreal leopard is capable of climbing trees at great speed and descending rapidly head first. It is also able to move along horizontal branches upside down. It hunts mainly at night. It feeds on squirrels, birds, monkeys, and other similar-sized animals. The gestation period lasts for about 90 days after which the female gives birth to between two and four cubs. The young have dark markings on their coats which become lighter as the cubs grow into adulthood.

Geographic distribution. India, Burma, Indochina, Borneo, Sumatra and Taiwan.

Habitat. In keeping with its tree-dwelling habits, the Clouded Leopard frequents evergreen forests which range from sea level to an altitude of 6,500ft (2,000m).

Population. This species has noticeably declined as a result of hunting for its fur and the destruction of its natural habitat for the development of agriculture. It is now protected over most of its range and a small number live in parks or reserves. The Clouded Leopard has been successfully bred in captivity.

SNOW LEOPARD
Panthera uncia

CLASS
Mammals

SUBCLASS
Eutheria

ORDER
Carnivora

SUBORDER
Fissipedia

FAMILY
Felidae

SUBFAMILY
Felinae

GENUS
Panthera

Description. The Snow Leopard can often measure over 6½ft (2m), including tail. It has a long thick coat which varies in colour from grey to cream, with rosettes of darker grey. It is mainly diurnal and hunts on its own – except during the mating season or during the rearing of cubs – when it is possible to see two or more hunting together. As fauna is thinly spread over its range, the Snow Leopard has to cover vast distances. In high altitudes it preys mainly on markhor, thar, and ibex; if necessary it will hunt birds and small mammals. In winter, when it descends to lower regions, it hunts wild boar, deer, and gazelles. The gestation period is about 100 days; between two and five cubs are born. In captivity the male also helps in the rearing of the young.

Geographic distribution. Its exact range is uncertain, it is present in the mountainous zones of central Asia. The southern limit of its range is northern India.

Habitat. Altitudes between 9,800 and 19,700ft (3,000 – 6,000m). In winter it descends into valleys between 4,900 and 6,500ft (1,500 – 2,000m).

Population. Exact numbers are unknown. It is believed that up to 100 could still be present in Pakistan. Although it is protected throughout most of its range, it is still hunted for its valuable skin. In 1971 the International Fur Trade Federation agreed to a voluntary ban amongst its membership on the use of Snow Leopard pelts, but this had little impact, and even in the 1980s they were still freely available in Kashmir. It is found in a number of zoos where it has reproduced successfully.

ASIATIC LION

Panthera leo persica

CLASS
Mammals

SUBCLASS
Eutheria

ORDER
Carnivora

SUBORDER
Fissipedia

FAMILY
Felidae

SUBFAMILY
Felinae

GENUS
Panthera

Description. Of all lions, the Asiatic or Indian Lion is in greatest danger of extinction. The differences between the Asiatic and African Lions are slight and have not warranted separate classification. However, geographically there is quite a lot of variation between individual African Lions: colouring, length of mane, and tail. The Asiatic Lion has a tawny coat; the mane varies in colour from tawny to black, but it is usually pale. The males are about 5½ft (1.70m) long; the tail measures a further 35 – 39in (90 – 100cm). The shoulder height is approximately 35in (90cm) and the weight is 400 – 440lb (180 – 200kg). Females are smaller. After a gestation period of three and a half months between two and four (sometimes five or six) dapple-coated cubs are born. The young are suckled for six to seven months, and the mane begins to appear in males at about 18 months. Lions usually live up to 15 years in the wild, but in captivity they can live as long as 25 years. One male African Lion in Cologne Zoo died aged 29. Lions live in prides of two or three males and five to ten females with their young. Contrary to popular belief, lionesses do not obtain food for the males, instead the males frequently seize a portion of the female's prey as they do with other carnivores (usually cheetahs). The male kills only a thirteenth of what he eats. The Asiatic Lion mainly preys upon the Nilgai Antelope, Axis Deer, Sambar, and wild boar. When these are scarce it frequently attacks domestic livestock; it also eats small mammals.

Geographic distribution. Until recently the Asiatic Lion was found over a large part of Asia Minor. It was common in Israel during biblical times, but has been extinct there since the thirteenth century. A hundred years ago it was still present in Iraq, Iran, and the whole of eastern India. It disappeared from Iraq and Iran between the First and Second World Wars (recent claimed sightings of the animal in Iran are questionable). Today the Asiatic Lion is limited to a single reserve in the forest of

Gir, covering an area of 450 sq miles (1,200 sq km) and its immediate vicinity in western India, to the north-west of Bombay.

Habitat. Unlike the African Lion, which is essentially an animal of the savannah, the Asiatic Lion prefers teak forests surrounded by dense acacia scrub interspersed with areas of cultivated land. During the rainy season many lions leave the forest to follow the cattle which feed on the grass in the open areas.

Population. The Indian Lions are descended from those killed by King David in the deserts of Palestine. Killed and hunted through the ages, it was reduced at the end of the last century to no more than 100 individuals confined to the forest of Gir and protected by the Nabob of Junagadh in whose state most of the forest lay. It was legally protected in 1900 and numbers increased from 100 to 289 in 1936. Unfortunately, the large amount of human settlement in this area meant that the forests were gradually being destroyed and livestock had eaten much of the vegetation on which the prey of the Asiatic Lion depended. In addition, the local inhabitants poisoned the lions in order to protect their livestock. The lion population, which had remained almost constant between 1936 and 1955, began to decline by 1968. Protective measures were strengthened and by 1973 the lion population was about 200. It was also noticeable that the number of deer, antelope and wild boar – the natural prey of the Asiatic Lion – had augmented. The Asiatic Lion population in the Gir Forest is at, or near, carrying capacity, and it is therefore important to establish other populations. In the late 1970s attempts were made to re-establish them in Iran, but in the subsequent political turmoil it is not clear as to the results. By 1990 there were well over 200 in captivity, most of which were bred from captive stock.

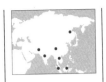

CLASS
Mammals

SUBCLASS
Eutheria

ORDER
Carnivora

SUBORDER
Fissipedia

FAMILY
Felidae

SUBFAMILY
Felinae

GENUS
Panthera

TIGER
Panthera tigris

Description. The Tiger is the national symbol of India and one of the best known animals in the world. It frequently appears in the literature and culture of the countries of its range as well as that of the Western World. This great cat – the largest of all felids – is lithe, strong, and has a powerful muscular body. It has strong solid limbs that are relatively long. The head has a marked bone structure and is heavier–looking than the lion's. Adult males can measure up to 10ft (3m). Females are slightly smaller. Males weigh up to 600lb (272kg). The Tiger has a perfect build for leaping and hunting. It has massive cervical and jaw muscles. The strong canine teeth allow the Tiger to bite and tear the toughest skin and sinews of its prey. The coat is basically tawny, but varies according to different subspecies. It has transversal black stripes (also varying in the different subspecies) on its sides, neck, limbs and head. The belly is almost pure white. The fur is generally smooth and short, slightly longer on the sides of the head, forming side whiskers in males. Tigers are carnivorous and generally hunt alone. It can kill an adult male buffalo, leaping on to its back, and using the powerful impact and strong forelegs to break the cervical column, causing the beast to fall down immobilized. Despite its awesome strength, the Tiger prefers deer, wild boar and other medium-sized animals, which are easy to hunt. If necessary it will also feed on lizards, frogs, mice and other small animals. Females reach sexual maturity at four years and will give birth to between two and four cubs. Usually only half or less will reach adulthood. In the wild the Tiger gives birth every two or three years. In the wild they can live up to 15 years, but often do not live so long.

Geographic distribution. The Tiger's range extends over the Indian subcontinent, surrounding islands, Indonesia and Asia.

Habitat. Found in a wide variety of habitats: tropical forest, savannah, swampland, and tundra up to an altitude of 7,900ft (2,400m). They like damp humid places where they can swim.

Population. In the 1930s the estimated population on the Indian subcontinent alone was 40,000. Today the species worldwide numbers less than 5,000 (including the different subspecies). The Indian subcontinent population is thought to be less than 2,000 today. The main reasons for this rapid decline are hunting for its highly-prized pelt and the destruction of the forests, particularly for valuable wood. The Tiger is now protected throughout its range. In the future it is unlikely that Tigers will survive outside national parks, sanctuaries, and other protected areas. Conflicts with human interests are common, and the Tiger is one of the few animals that includes man as a regular item of prey. Although in a few reserves tiger populations flourish, in most areas they are declining. They breed freely in captivity but many captive populations are of mixed origins, and there is virtually no prospect of any being reintroduced into the wild.

CLASS
Mammals

SUBCLASS
Eutheria

ORDER
Perissodactyla

SUBORDER
Hippomorpha

FAMILY
Equidae

GENUS
Equus

PRZEWALSKI'S WILD HORSE

Equus przewalskii

Description. Przewalski's Wild Horse stands about 4½ft (1.40m) at the shoulders and measures 9ft (2.80m) in length. It weighs between 440 – 660lb (200 – 300kg). The long-haired tail is approximately 3ft (1m) long. Its mane differs from other horses in that it is stiff and erect, about 6 – 8in (15 – 20cm) long, and lacking a forelock. The body is golden red or golden brown on the upper parts and whitish on the underneath and muzzle; the mane, tail and legs are brownish-black. The dark stripe on its back is hardly noticeable. In winter the colour deepens slightly and the coat becomes longer and thicker. Its head is large with a short stumpy neck. In common with domestic horses, the female gives birth to one foal after a gestation period of about 330 days; the foal is suckled for six or seven months. The species can live for up to 28 years, although some in captivity have lived longer – one female born in Philadelphia Zoo and transferred to Washington Zoo died aged 33. It can be crossed with the domestic horse. It has also been crossed with the zebra, but sterile crossbreeds were produced. Attempts at crossing it with the ass have been unsuccessful. Little is recorded of the species' behaviour in the wild; they spend the day in desert territory and at dusk move to pastureland where there is water, returning to the desert after dawn. The few herds that have been observed consist of a maximum of 20, led by an adult male who positions himself at the back of the herd when danger arises, acting as a rearguard. They feed on tough grasses which the domestic horse would reject. Foals are born between April and May. A very small number of Przewalski's Horses have been trained and ridden, but in general it is not possible to tame them.

Geographic distribution. It is thought that in prehistoric times Przewalski's Horse inhabited a vast area, with a subspecies in western Europe. At the time of its discovery in 1879 it was already very rare and only inhabited the steppes on the borders of Mongolia and China (Dzungaria and the Gobi Desert). Now it only inhabits an area of 250 sq miles (650 sq km) between the Takhin Shar-nuru and Baitag-Gogdo mountain ranges.

Habitat. Southern slopes of high mountains and steppes in autumn and winter; semi-desert areas in spring and summer. It depends on natural water sources but has to compete with local nomadic tribes and their livestock. These timid horses are therefore driven into more and more remote areas.

Population. Przewalski's Horse was discovered in 1879 in the Gobi Desert by the famous Russian explorer, Nikolai Przewalski. The animal was then studied by the Russian zoologist I.S. Poliakov, who established that it was not a Tarpan but a new species and named it after its discoverer. The population, which was not very large at the time of its discovery was drastically reduced between 1930 and 1950 as a result of poor pasture and frozen terrain (especially between 1948 and 1956). It was further diminished by political disturbances and frequent border conflicts. It became extinct in the wild in the 1970s despite protection in Mongolia since 1926. However, there are thriving captive populations and by the end of the 1980s serious consideration was being given to establishing reintroduction programmes. By the late 1980s more than 100 zoos and other animal collections maintained Przewalski's Horses, and there were more than 600 in captivity at the end of 1986.

CLASS
Mammals

SUBCLASS
Eutheria

ORDER
Perissodactyla

SUBORDER
Hippomorpha

FAMILY
Equidae

GENUS
Equus

ASIATIC WILD ASS
Equus hemionus

Description. Two of the five subspecies are in danger of extinction; the Syrian Wild Ass (*Equus hemionus hemippus*) and the Indian Wild Ass (the Khur) (*E.h. khur*). The three other subspecies are the Kulan (*E.h. hemionus*), the Onager (*E.h. onager*) and the Kiang (*E.h. kiang*), illustrated opposite, which is usually considered to be a separate species. These wild Asian Equidae are similar to both the ass and horse, though unlike the horse only the tip of the tail is covered with hair and the ears are similar to those of the African Wild Ass. Of the five subspecies, the Kiang is the largest, reaching a shoulder height of 5ft (1.50m), and weighing 775 – 880lb (350 – 400kg). Asiatic Wild Asses are gregarious and graze in herds led by a female. By day they search for food, eating plants and salty grasses in the hill country, and by night shelter beneath shrubs. When resting or grazing the herd is well spaced for maximum security, so that it covers as large an area as possible while remaining a group. They can reach a galloping speed of 45 miles (70km) per hour but their normal speed, which can be maintained for long distances, is about 25 – 30 miles (40 – 50km) per hour. Unlike the African Wild Ass, Asiatic Wild Asses are very dependent on water, visiting a watering place once or twice a day, preferably at dawn and sunset. There is no mating season as this depends on the environmental and seasonal conditions of each of the many areas it inhabits. The gestation period is 11 months. The foal is protected and cared for by its mother for the first two weeks; it is then able to follow the herd.

Geographic distribution. Asiatic Wild Asses were found from Arabia to Tibet. The distribution of the two subspecies can be traced as follows: the Syrian Wild Ass found its way through Syria, Palestine, Arabia and Iraq. It is probably extinct. The Indian Wild Ass, the Khur, was numerous throughout north-west India and west Pakistan. Now the major area of distribution is a small desert zone of about 1,000 sq miles (2,590 sq km) along the Pakistan/Gujaret border.

Habitat. Desert and sub-desert areas with sparse shrub vegetation; the Khur also inhabits desert areas rich in salt.

Population. The Syrian Wild Ass is now believed to be extinct. Those that inhabited the greater Syrian desert have probably been extinct for 20 to 30 years. It was wiped out in northern Syria by the local Anazeh and Shamnar tribesmen. The Khur numbered between 3,000 and 5,000 in 1946; 870 in 1962; 400 in October 1969 and by December 1969 the number had decreased to a total of 368. Its population was estimated at 2,000 in 1984. Asiatic Wild Asses are kept in many zoos.

CLASS
Mammals

SUBCLASS
Eutheria

ORDER
Perissodactyla

SUBORDER
Ceratomorpha

FAMILY
Rhinocerotidae

GENUS
Rhinoceros

INDIAN RHINOCEROS
Rhinoceros unicornis

Description. Like the Javan Rhinoceros, the Indian Rhinoceros is distinguished from the African Rhinoceros by the loose folds of skin, or armour, as they have been described since antiquity. This loose skin is covered with horny tubercles and drapes over the shoulders. The skin is completely hairless apart from the ears and tip of the tail. The tough hide is as thick as an elephant's. An adult male can reach up to 13ft (4m) in length, including a 24-in (60-cm) tail. It can weigh over two tons. It has a single horn. Despite its massive bulk the Indian Rhinoceros trots and gallops at speeds of up to 28 miles (40km) per hour. It has only three toes on each foot with huge nails separated by fleshy cushions. Its two sharp incisors are a particularly effective weapon if attacked. Like all rhinoceroses, the Indian Rhinoceros is vegetarian and eats grasses, shoots, reeds and leaves. It tears off the leaves from the higher branches with its flexible specially adapted upper lip which is rather like a small proboscis. In captivity they are fed on fruit, carrots, grain pellets and vitamins. According to information gathered from a number of zoos, the Indian Rhinoceros will consume 44 – 55lb (20 – 25kg) of dry foodstuffs each day, and drink up to 26gal (100l) of water. Studies of the Indian Rhinoceros in the wild have shown it not to be a particularly solitary animal: single animals have been sighted, but also groups of several individuals. Nor is it confined to a rigid territory. It wanders over vast distances within its habitat in search of food and safe areas. Occasionally there will be fighting over territory and scars are left on the tough hides. The Indian Rhinoceros does not appear to have natural enemies; no animal dares attack. However, it will retreat from the elephant, though a female is prepared to take one on if the safety of her young is threatened. The mating season is between February and April. The gestation period is 16 months. Newborn young weigh about 143lb (65kg) and have no horn.

Geographic distribution. The species once inhabited a large area of northern India and Nepal: from the foothills of the Hindu Kush Mountains to the west of Peshawar, and to the southern bush area of the River Indus to the south of Kashmir, and all along the Himalayan foothills as far as Burma. Today it is limited to the Brahmaputra Valley in Assam, Jaldapara, and Gorumara in West Bengal, and the Rapti Valley region of Nepal.

Habitat. The Indian Rhinoceros prefers plains covered with tall grasses and shrubs, and swampy areas with lakes and streams where it can wallow in the mud. Today, particularly in Nepal, many of these rhinoceroses live in the forest and graze in cultivated areas.

Population. By the late 1950s it was estimated that around 400 survived in India, the majority in Kaziranga Sanctuary, Assam. There were also about 300 in Nepal. Under protection the numbers have increased slowly and were over 1,000 by the early 1980s. Small numbers are maintained in zoos, with an increasing proportion captive-bred.

CLASS
Mammals

SUBCLASS
Eutheria

ORDER
Perissodactyla

SUBORDER
Ceratomorpha

FAMILY
Rhinocerotidae

GENUS
Rhinoceros

JAVAN OR LESSER ONE–HORNED RHINOCEROS

Rhinoceros sondaicus

Description. The Javan Rhinoceros differs from the Indian Rhinoceros in that it is slightly smaller with one of the characteristic folds of loose skin meeting over the shoulders. The horn is also very small in the male and virtually nonexistent in the female. The head is slimmer and longer with a slightly extended upper lip. An adult can measure 10ft (3m) in length, including tail, with a shoulder height of 4½ft (1.40m). Not much is known about its habits, but its diet is similar to that of the Indian Rhinoceros – shoots and leaves of shrubs which it tears off with its flexible upper lip. The Javan Rhinoceros reaches maturity very quickly and adults are not gregarious.

Geographic distribution. Once distributed over a large part of India, Bangladesh, Burma, Thailand, Cambodia, Laos, Vietnam, the Malaysian Peninsula, and the islands of Sumatra and Java. It is certainly present in the Udjong-Kulon Reserve at the extreme western tip of Java.

Habitat. It prefers areas of dense vegetation: forests and high mountain forests, marshy areas, and coastal zones.

Population. In 1950 the Javan Rhinoceros was still present in the Sunderbans, the Brahmaputra Valley, and the Chittagong Hills, but probably extinct by the 1960s. By the 1980s the only viable population was in the Udjong-Kulon Reserve in Java. It is one of the rarest mammals in the world, and by the late 1980s its total population had fallen to less than 50 individuals, and last-ditch attempts were being made to maintain a captive stock.

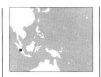

SUMATRAN RHINOCEROS
Dicerorhinus sumatrensis

CLASS
Mammals

SUBCLASS
Eutheria

ORDER
Perissodactyla

SUBORDER
Ceratomorpha

FAMILY
Rhinocerotidae

GENUS
Dicerorhinus

Description. The Sumatran Rhinoceros, the only species of its genus, is the smallest living rhinoceros. It is the least developed and the only one whose body is partly covered in coarse hair. Its total length hardly measures 10ft (3m), its height is 4½ft (1.40m), and its weight just one ton. While all the other Asian rhinoceroses have a single horn, the Sumatran Rhinoceros has two. In the male, the first horn measures up to 23in (60cm) and the second 8in (20cm); the females' horns are much smaller, and the second is a mere bump. The hair is long and rough. Even the ears are fringed with hair, although it is less thick in the adult. The skin is covered with small lumps and the folds of skin are not as loose as in the Javan Rhinoceros. The Sumatran Rhinoceros is basically nocturnal and lives alone or in small groups, wandering in search of bamboo shoots and leaves.

Geographic distribution. It was once found equally distributed throughout South-east Asia.

Habitat. This species prefers huge tropical forest, bush, swamps and reed beds with rich vegetation, from the low plains to a height of 6,500ft (2,000m).

Population. This species is in grave danger of extinction due to its very small population. However, the populations, probably all of one or two animals, are all widely scattered and isolated from each other. It is rather unlikely that the species will survive into the twenty-first century. It is protected throughout its range.

WILD CAMEL
Camelus bactrianus

CLASS
Mammals

SUBCLASS
Eutheria

ORDER
Artiodactyla

SUBORDER
Tylopoda

FAMILY
Camelidae

GENUS
Camelus

Description. Compared to the domestic camel, the Wild, or Bactrian Camel is slimmer and less hairy with smaller feet and smaller humps. During the heat of the summer the herds move up to the mountain zones as high as 10,000ft (3,000m); in winter they return to the desert. The young are born in March after a gestation period of 13 months.
Geographic distribution. Up to 1920 the species was numerous in the Gobi Desert, in Mongolia and Turkestan.
Habitat. The Gobi Desert, semi-desert and steppes.
Population. Enormously diminished because of intensive hunting and from competition with domestic livestock. The species was considered to be extinct but in the 1980s there were estimated to be 300 – 500 in the Gobi Desert on the Sino-Mongolian border.

PERSIAN FALLOW DEER
Dama mesopotamica

CLASS
Mammals

SUBCLASS
Eutheria

ORDER
Artiodactyla

SUBORDER
Ruminantia

FAMILY
Cervidae

SUBFAMILY
Cervinae

GENUS
Dama

Description. The Persian Fallow Deer is notably larger than the European Common Fallow Deer (*Dama dama*). It can measure 41in (105cm) at the withers and weigh 440lb (200kg).
Geographic distribution. Previously distributed from Syria and Palestine as far as Iraq and Iran. Now it is only found in two restricted zones in Iran, on the banks of the Dez and Karkheh rivers.
Habitat. Thick areas of vegetation.
Population. The species was thought to be extinct in 1917 and then rediscovered in 1955. The species is now protected in Iran and the two zones it inhabits are now national parks. Its current status is unknown, but there are small herds in captivity, with a large group in Hai-Bar, Israel.

BROW-ANTLERED DEER OR THAMIN
Cervus eldi

CLASS
Mammals

SUBCLASS
Eutheria

ORDER
Artiodactyla

SUBORDER
Ruminantia

FAMILY
Cervidae

SUBFAMILY
Cervinae

GENUS
Cervus

Description. This south-east Asian deer can be divided into three subspecies: Thamin or Eld's Deer (*C.e. thamin*), Sangai or Manipur Eld's Deer (*C.e. eldi*) and Siamese Eld's Deer (*C.e. siamensis*). The species is about 43–45in (110–115cm) high, 43in (108cm) long and weighs up to 330lb (150kg). The males have a dark brown winter coat with a whitish belly; in summer, the dark brown colour lightens and the belly becomes darker. The females always keep the same yellow-brown colouring.

Geographic distribution. The subspecies inhabit the countries from which they get their names.

Habitat. Copses and plains with water.

Population. This deer is in great danger of extinction because of intensive hunting: the Manipur subspecies, which is the rarest, is slowly increasing from a low of 14 in 1975 in a reserve of 14sq miles (35sq km).

FORMOSAN SIKA
Cervus nippon taiouanus

CLASS
Mammals

SUBCLASS
Eutheria

ORDER
Artiodactyla

SUBORDER
Ruminantia

FAMILY
Cervidae

SUBFAMILY
Cervinae

GENUS
Cervus

Description. The Sika is a medium-sized deer and compactly built with a slender head and dappled coat. Its shoulder height is about 30–43in (75–110cm) and its length 41–45in (105–115cm). It weighs about 243lb (110kg). There are several subspecies, five of which are in danger of extinction.

Geographic distribution. From Siberia across Manchuria and eastern China to Indochina; Japan and Taiwan.

Habitat. Scrubland and mountain forests.

Population. The Formosan Sika: probably numbers less than 300, but there are many more in captivity where they have been successfully bred.

CLASS
Mammals

SUBCLASS
Eutheria

ORDER
Artiodactyla

SUBORDER
Ruminantia

FAMILY
Cervidae

SUBFAMILY
Cervinae

GENUS
Elaphurus

PÈRE DAVID'S DEER

Elaphurus davidianus

Description. Père David's Deer is the only representative of the genus *Elaphurus*, and believed to originate in China. This large deer can measure up to 5ft (1.50m) in length and stand 4ft (1.20m) at the shoulders. It weighs about 440lb (200kg). Its long tail is more like that of a horse. The antlers divide just above the head into two branches. Père David's Deer was only recently discovered. In 1865 a French missionary, Father Armand David, was en route for Peking and heard about a wonderful nature park belonging to the emperor at Na-Hai-Tzu, only a short distance from Peking. A passionate zoologist, Father David desperately wanted to visit this park in spite of a protective wall 45 miles (72km) long and guards stationed along it. He escaped the surveillance of these guards, climbed on top of the wall and was able to view all the things he had heard about. His attention was immediately caught by a species of deer he had never encountered before. On returning to Peking, he asked all the local experts for information and learnt that these animals were occasionally killed by the Mongolian guards for meat, or very rarely, to sell the antlers. In 1866, after many unsuccessful attempts, Father David obtained two hides. Shortly afterwards the French delegation in Peking obtained two living specimens, but these died before reaching Paris. The naturalist, Milne-Edwards, studied the remains and gave a scientific classification of the deer: in honour of Father David, he named it *Elaphurus davidianus*. The only existing examples lived in the park near Peking as they had already become extinct in the wild. In 1869 and 1883 four deer were sent to the Zoological Society in London: one was also sent to Berlin. The Duke of Bed-

ford, another passionate zoologist, obtained 18 for his park at Woburn Abbey. This was the salvation of the species: a few years later, in 1895, the River Hun He flooded its banks causing part of the protective wall surrounding the park to collapse. Most of the deer that escaped were killed by the starving population; a small number survived inside the park but were later killed by troops occupying Peking after the Boxer Rebellion in 1900. Only one female survived; it died in Peking in 1920. Therefore, the only surviving examples of the species were at Woburn Abbey, England, for the next few decades.

Geographic distribution. The orginal distribution is believed to have been the central and northern regions of China. Fossils have also been discovered in Manchuria and in Japan.

Habitat. Wet or marshy areas, as the large, spreading hooves indicate.

Population. It is not certain what the population of this species was in the nineteenth century in the Peking park, perhaps only a few hundred examples. By 1932 there were already 182 at Woburn Abbey, and steadily increasing. By the 1980s, with more than 1,000 individuals worldwide in zoos and parks, a semi-wild group had been established in China.

CLASS
Mammals

SUBCLASS
Eutheria

ORDER
Perissodactyla

SUBORDER
Ceratomorpha

FAMILY
Tapiridae

GENUS
Tapirus

MALAYAN TAPIR
Tapirus indicus

Description. The Malayan Tapir, also known as the Indian Tapir, differs from the three species, found in Central and South America, in its rather strange colouring. Its coat is dark, almost black, with a striking wide band of pale grey stretching over the back and beneath the belly, rather like a saddle. Young Malayan Tapirs are brownish and at two months develop longitudinal white stripes with alternate bands of white blotches. These disappear by five months. This species is larger than the American species, and can reach a total length of 8ft (2.50m). The Tapir's diet is very varied; although it prefers young shoots, leaves, and tender branches of certain shrubby plants, it will also eat fruit and grasses. Unsociable by nature, Tapirs keep to the same area, making tracks in the undergrowth through constant use.

Geographic distribution. Its range extends from south Burma, through Thailand, the Malay Peninsula to Sumatra.

Habitat. This Tapir, like the other species, inhabits humid, tropical forest, particularly near rivers, lakes and swamps.

Population. In spite of the worrying reduction of the species' numbers in recent years, its overall area of distribution has not appreciably reduced. It is still present in protected areas in Thailand, although in much smaller numbers. It was hunted there mainly for its meat which was highly valued and until recently sold in markets. Hunting is less of a problem in Sumatra and Malaysia as the local Muslim population consider the meat impure. However, the species is in serious danger of extinction in these areas where their habitat is being developed for agriculture and they are being forced into remoter areas. It is now illegal to hunt it in all the countries of its range. They are often kept in zoos where they breed freely.

TAMARAW
Bubalus (Anoa) mindorensis

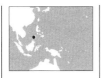

CLASS
Mammals

SUBCLASS
Eutheria

ORDER
Artiodactyla

SUBORDER
Ruminantia

FAMILY
Bovidae

SUBFAMILY
Bovinae

GENUS
Bubalus

Description. According to some authorities, the Tamaraw belongs to the subgenus *Bubalus*; according to others, to the subgenus *Anoa*. The main difference is its smaller size. It has the same light stripes across its throat and above the hooves. It is probable that these two species developed their own particular characteristics as they inhabit two separate islands in the Philippines: the Tamaraw is found on Mindoro and the Anoa on Sulawesi.

Geographic distribution. Once distributed throughout Mindoro, today it is only found on Mount Iglit and Mount Baco, the Calavita mountains and the Sablayon region.

Habitat. The Tamaraw prefers primary forest which once covered the entire island.

Population. By the mid 1970s the population was estimated at 200 – 280 in the Mount Iglit Game Reserve, but it also occurred in other protected areas. Virtually nothing is known of the status of the Anoa on Sulawesi.

WILD YAK
Bos grunniens

CLASS
Mammals

SUBCLASS
Eutheria

ORDER
Artiodactyla

SUBORDER
Ruminantia

FAMILY
Bovidae

SUBFAMILY
Bovinae

GENUS
Bos

Description. The male can reach a shoulder height of 6ft (1.90m) and weigh more than 1,540lb (700kg). The female is much smaller. The Wild Yak has long, shaggy, blackish brown hair. It grazes on grasses. It has now become domesticated in some mountain areas.

Geographic distribution. It once inhabited a vast area of the Himalayas up to 14,800ft (4,500m). Today it is limited to the high plains of Tibet and neighbouring areas, from Ladakh in the east to Kuenlun and Kansu.

Habitat. Alpine Tundra; the vast deserted regions of high mountain.

Population. Numbers have declined drastically due to uncontrolled hunting. It is officially protected by the Chinese and Indian governments.

TAKIN
Budorcas taxicolor

Description. The Takin is a strange animal distantly related to the musk ox. It looks much like an ox with its large head and muzzle. With a shoulder height of up to 4ft (1.20m), it weighs up to 705lb (320kg). The short, sturdy legs have large rounded hooves. Both sexes have horns. The thick tough coat varies in colour: the Assam Takin (*Budorcas taxicolor taxicolor*, illustrated left) is golden-yellow to a ruddy brown with black patches; the Szechwan Takin (*Budorcas taxicolor tibetanus*) is yellow to reddish or silver-grey with black spots; the Golden Takin (*Budorcas taxicolor bedfordi*) is whitish yellow to gold. The mating season is in July and August; after a seven- to eight-month gestation period, one young is born which is able to follow its mother after a few days. They feed on bamboo and grasses.

Geographic distribution. The Assam Takin lives in the mountains of Nepal, Assam and Bhutan; the Szechwan Takin inhabits the Chinese province of that name, and the Golden Takin lives on the Great White Mountain, a sacred Chinese mountain in the southern part of the Shansi Province.

Habitat. Inaccessible mountain regions between 8,200 – 14,760ft (2,500 – 4,500m) in dense rhododendron and bamboo woodland. The Takin lives in small groups which descend to the more sheltered valleys in winter; in summer it lives on high grassland, making tracks through the thick undergrowth.

Population. The Szechwan and the Golden Takins are particularly rare due to intensive hunting for their meat. It is estimated that they number about 200. They are strongly protected by Chinese law but in order to ensure their survival it has been necessary to set up reserves in the regions they inhabit. Although not numerous in zoos, they breed regularly.

BANTENG

Bos javanicus

CLASS
Mammals

SUBCLASS
Eutheria

ORDER
Artiodactyla

SUBORDER
Ruminantia

FAMILY
Bovidae

SUBFAMILY
Bovinae

GENUS
Bos

Description. According to some authorities the Banteng can be divided into three subspecies; the Javan Banteng (*Bos j. javanicus*), the Borneo Banteng (*B.j. lowi*) and the Burmese Banteng (*B.j. birmanicus*). The Javan Banteng is slightly smaller with longer legs and can grow to a length of 6½ft (2m) and a height of 5½ft (1.70m). It weighs a maximum of 1,980lb (900kg). The males differ substantially from the females both in bulk and colouring. The male is usually dark brown with shades of black or very dark blue. The female is a brownish red. Bantengs live in herds composed of a few males and about 30 to 40 females.

Geographic distribution. At one time the species was distributed throughout Burma and Thailand across the Malaccan Peninsula to the islands of Java and Borneo; only a few fossils have been found on Sumatra. The species currently inhabits its original territories but in limited areas and in greatly reduced numbers. The domestic form lives ferally in Australia.

Habitat. Wooded areas, forests, hills, and mountains up to a height of 6,500ft (2,000m). It spends the monsoon season on the hills; in the dry season it descends into the valleys which are rich in vegetation.

Population. Although protected throughout its range, the Javan Banteng is greatly reduced in number due to poaching and the transformation of its natural habitat into agricultural land. The Banteng has been domesticated in Bali and Java although the domestic strain is slightly different from the wild variety. There are many in captivity, mostly descended from captive stock.

NILGIRI TAHR
Hemitragus hylocrius

CLASS
Mammals

SUBCLASS
Eutheria

ORDER
Artiodactyla

SUBORDER
Ruminantia

FAMILY
Bovidae

SUBFAMILY
Caprinae

GENUS
Hemitragus

Description. There are three species: the Himalayan Tahr (*Hemitragus jemlahicus*), the Arabian Tahr (*H. jayakari*) and the Nilgiri Tahr (*H. hylocrius*). The Nilgiri Tahr is the largest of the three species, with a shoulder height of 3ft (1m) and weighing 230lb (105kg). The Tahr has a long, soft shaggy coat with a slight mane. The male is a dark yellow colour, the females and young are more grey. The adult male has an off-white, saddle-like patch on the back. One young is born after a gestation period of six to eight months; the Nilgiri Tahr often gives birth to two offspring.

Geographic distribution. The Nilgiri Tahr once inhabited a large part of the mountainous regions of southern India. Today it is limited to a very restricted area in the extreme south and a few peaks of the Western Ghats mountains among the Nilgiri foothills from which it takes its name. The Arabian Tahr, whose original habitat was throughout the mountains and hills of Oman, is now limited to the mountains of Jobal Hafit and Jalan Shar Keeyeh at the extreme eastern tip.

Habitat. Monsoon region: the Nilgiri Tahr inhabits scrubland and grassy wooded areas between 4,000 and 6,000ft (1,200 and 1,830m).

Population. Both the Nilgiri Tahr and the Arabian Tahr are in serious danger due to excessive hunting and the destruction of their habitat. By the mid 1970s the population was estimated at only 2,230. The species is protected and four reserves have been set up. The Arabian Tahr is not protected; its population was estimated at less than 2,000 in the 1970s with an isolated population of c. 20 in the United Arab Emirates.

MARKHOR
Capra falconeri

CLASS
Mammals

SUBCLASS
Eutheria

ORDER
Artiodactyla

SUBORDER
Ruminantia

FAMILY
Bovidae

SUBFAMILY
Caprinae

GENUS
Capra

Description. There are six subspecies of Markhor which are distinguished by the shape of their horns; the Astor Markhor (*Capra falconeri falconeri*, illustrated below) has broadly spiralled horns. The Markhor is the largest and heaviest of the wild goats: the adult male can grow to a shoulder height of 3½ft (1.15m) and weigh 243lb (110kg). The horns of the male often exceed 5ft (1.50m) in length; the female's are the same shape but short (a maximum of 10in (25cm). Old males are distinguished by their long thick beards. The coat is soft and silky, shorter and yellowish brown in summer, becoming longer and greyish in winter. The mating season is in winter. One or two kids are born between the end of April and the beginning of June after a gestation period of six months.

Geographic distribution. The Markhor once inhabited the mountains from eastern Iran along the Afghanistan/Turkestan/Pakistan borders to Soviet Turkestan and Indian Kashmir. Today it is found in isolated areas of the West Himalayas.

Habitat. Steppes, forests and grasslands, rocky slopes between 5,900 and 9,800ft (1,800 and 3,000m).

Population. The Markhor has been drastically reduced in numbers through uncontrolled hunting and rivalry from domestic goats. The total population of all six subspecies was estimated between 2,000 and 2,500 in the 1970s, but it appears this was on the low side, and under protection they have increased in the Soviet Union. The Markhor adapts well to living in captivity, and has been self-sustaining for many years.

LION-TAILED MACAQUE
Macaca silenus

CLASS
Mammals

SUBCLASS
Eutheria

ORDER
Primates

SUBORDER
Simiae

FAMILY
Cercopithecidae

GENUS
Macaca

Description. Although not the largest representative of the *Macaca* genus, this monkey reaches a considerable size: the male is 3ft (1m) long and the female 2½ft (78cm); the tail takes up about two fifths of this overall length. The coat is distinctive, in strongly contrasting black and white. The whole appearance of the animal is striking because of the luxuriant beard covering most of the face, and the alert and vivid expression of its bright brown eyes. The Lion-tailed Macaque's behaviour is similar to the majority of the tree-living species of the genus. The old classic works based their descriptions on accounts obtained from the local Indian population which were largely influenced by myth and religion.

Geographic distribution. In 1859 the species extended from Goa to Cape Comorin, occupying the entire region of western Ghats. Even then – according to contemporary accounts – it was limited to the remote forest zones, which were more widespread and numerous. Basically the area has not changed much. There is no precise data on the species being present north of 11° latitude North. Only one valid record gives a sighting on Anshi Ghat between Kadra and Kumbharwada (15° latitude North) at an altitude of c. 1,000ft (c. 300m) above sea level.

Habitat. Evergreen forest up to an altitude of 2,000 ft (600m) above sea level. The species is restricted to a certain type of habitat and its existence relies on particular ecological conditions.

Population. A species seriously in danger. From data obtained from one section of their area (between 9°30′N and 11°30′N) and then applied proportionately to the whole area, it was estimated in 1968 that there were no more than 1,000. The numbers are still falling despite various measures taken to safeguard them. Several factors have contributed to the virtual destruction of the macaque: agricultural expansion of the tea and coffee plantations; the felling of trees to meet industrial demands for timber and for use by the local inhabitants as fuel; the replacement of trees and shrubs by fast growing ones, such as eucalyptus, which are not indigenous to the Indian continent. Hunting, above all, has taken its toll – not only by catching the young macaques but also by killing the adults, especially the females. There was a commercial demand for the monkeys – charming as pets, they are especially endearing when young – but this has been stopped, mainly because their importation has been banned by the USA, formerly one of the most important markets. The hunting of all monkeys, including the Lion-tailed Macaque, has been banned in Madras, thus affording the species real protection. In the Periyar Wildlife Sanctuary too, it has found shelter and is said to be doing very well, although it has been reported that there is a high incidence of poaching. To ensure the survival of the species a comprehensive study of its ecology must be carried out to assess its tolerance to changes and environment, and consequently to calculate the effect of the introduction of exotic vegetation, and containing it accordingly. By 1975 the population had fallen to under 400. Their main stronghold, the Silent Valley (Bhavani River), is threatened by proposals to develop hydro-electricity. Although these have been rejected so far, the threat may reappear.

CLASS
Mammals

SUBCLASS
Eutheria

ORDER
Primates

SUBORDER
Simiae

FAMILY
Pongidae

GENUS
Pongo

ORANG-UTAN
Pongo pygmaeus

Description. This is the only great ape in Asia and one of the most intelligent of the primates. The front limbs are very long, with large hands and strong fingers. The finger bones are curved to ensure a better grip on branches. The hind limbs are short. Orang-utans can measure 5ft 10in (180cm) in height. The average male stands about 4ft 5ins (137cm) tall; the females are shorter, and can be half the weight. The male Sumatran Orang-utan weighs around 155lb (70kg) and the female 83lb (37kg); the male from Borneo weighs up to 418lb (189kg) and the female 178lb (80kg). The hair is long; in the adult male it forms full side-whiskers together with a moustache and beard. The Orang-utan is a tawny, reddish yellow; the face is grey. The adult male develops a large throat sac connected to the larynx, which aids voice projection. The Orang-utan lives in families of two to four; sometimes an isolated male will live alone. They are tranquil animals, silent and usually shy. They move through the trees, mainly by swinging along branches. Their movements are agile. The adults move with slow assurance and without haste. On the ground the Orang-utan goes along on the knuckles of the hand and the lateral edge of the feet. Mating takes place at any time of the year. The gestation period is nine months. The new born young weighs a little under 3lb (1.5kg). Maturity is reached at seven to ten years and the lifespan may be 40 years or more. One pair in Philadelphia Zoo were 56 years old when they died.

Geographic distribution. Sumatra (Atjeh, to the north of the Wampoe river, along the Simpang-Kanan and Peureulak rivers, the eastern coast between Menlaboh and Singkel) and Borneo (Sabah, Sandakan, Sarawak between the Sadong and the Butang Lupar rivers, to the south of the Rajang and Balek rivers, sources of the Balui and the Baram Kalimantan).

Habitat. Tree forest in the primary and secondary tropical rain forest.

Population. Since the 1930s their range in Sumatra has decreased by about 30 per cent, and by the 1970s the world population may have been as low as 5,000. The species is in serious danger as a result of radical changes to its habitat and from hunting. The forest has been cleared for agricultural purposes and trees are being felled for timber. Mechanization has not only speeded these operations but has inflicted far more damage than the axe to the animals' habitat. The Orang-utan does not adapt to conditions outside its natural habitat. If this is destroyed or altered, the species will be unable to survive. The Orang-utan is protected by law. There are a number of reserves in Sarawak, Sabah and Indonesia. The question of reintroducing on to reserves Orang-utans confiscated from illegal hunters has been studied. But the capture of Orang-utans — involving the killing of the mothers so as to take the young — continues in the remote areas. Besides this illegal trade, the slaughter of the animals for food has not been effectively prevented. In short, although conservation measures exist, they are inadequate. What is needed is not so much new schemes but the more efficient operation of the present ones. In the 1970s publicity led to a reduction in the number of wild-caught Orang-utans being imported by zoos. There are now large numbers in captivity and many are bred each year.

INDUS DOLPHIN
Platanista indi

CLASS
Mammals

SUBCLASS
Eutheria

ORDER
Cetacea

SUBORDER
Odontoceti

FAMILY
Platanistidae

GENUS
Platanista

Description. The Indus Dolphin differs from the similar Ganges Dolphin only in some characteristics of the skull. The Indus Dolphin is only 7 − 10ft (2 −3m) long, but there is a record of a female of 13ft (4m). The eyes are very small, the pectoral fins are short and fan−shaped, the dorsal fin is flattened. The long slender snout is 7 − 8in (18 − 20cm) long. There are 28 − 29 teeth on each side of the jaw-bones. It is lead to blackish grey in colour, the underneath being slightly lighter. A freshwater dolphin, it comes up for air at 30-second to two-minute intervals. Strange and inoffensive, it lives in groups of three to ten or even more. Being blind, it searches for fish, crustaceans and other organisms on the river-bed by means of its sensitive snout. The female produces one offspring after a gestation period of eight or nine months. At birth the young is about 18in (45cm) long and weighs 15lb (7kg).

Geographic distribution. Until the mid-dle of the nineteenth century the dolphin was spread throughout the Indus in Pakistan and its principal tributaries as far as the river mouth. Now it is restricted to limited parts of the Indus, especially between the Sukkur and Kotri dams, and in the artificial basins created by dams in the tributary. They are sometimes also found in irrigation canals.

Habitat. The species prefers murky water where the river current is rather slow. By day they stay in deep water, but at night they go to the shallower water near the banks to search for fish and shrimps. Their habitat has been progressively reduced because of the increasing amount of water which is being drawn from the rivers for irrigation and hydroelectricity.

Population. The number of surviving Indus Dolphins has been estimated at around 400. It has been protected in some zones since the early 1970s but is still occasionally hunted by fishermen, and is sometimes caught in their nets.

DOUC LANGUR
Pygathrix nemaeus

CLASS
Mammals

SUBCLASS
Eutheria

ORDER
Primates

SUBORDER
Simiae

FAMILY
Cercopithecidae

GENUS
Pygathrix

Description. This monkey has an overall length of 44 – 48in (117 – 152cm), including a 23 – 30-in (56 – 76-cm) tail. Very little is known about this brightly coloured, yellow-faced species.
Geographic distribution. Laos, Vietnam and the island of Hainan; but little is known of their precise range.
Habitat. A forest dweller, this monkey inhabits tropical rain forest up to altitudes of 6,650ft (2,000m).
Population. No recent data available. Much of its habitat has suffered in Vietnam and Laos because of bombing, fire and general warfare. Many were killed for food. Although protected in Vietnam, little is known of its status.

GREAT INDIAN BUSTARD
Ardeotis nigriceps

CLASS
Aves

SUBCLASS
Neornithes

ORDER
Gruiformes

FAMILY
Otididae

GENUS
Ardeotis

Description. The Great Indian Bustard is one of the largest flying birds in the world. Standing upright, it reaches a height of 3ft (1m) with a wingspan of 8ft (2.50m) and a weight of 44lb (20kg). It lives in small groups which rarely exceed ten individuals. A single egg is laid, and incubation is believed to take a long time. The bird perfoms a useful function in destroying grasshoppers and small animals that harm vegetation.
Geographic distribution. India: from the Punjab to Deccan and Sind in the south, and as far as the River Jumna in the east.
Habitat. Open, grassy areas.
Population. Exact population unknown, although it is an endangered species. The reasons for its decline are the destruction of its habitat and the fact that it is still hunted in spite of legal protection. However, in the late 1980s the population was believed stable.

SHORT-TAILED ALBATROSS
Diomedea albatrus

CLASS
Aves

SUBCLASS
Neornithes

ORDER
Procellariformes

FAMILY
Diomedeidae

GENUS
Diomedea

Description. The Short-tailed Albatross, also known as Steller's Albatross, is white with dark wings: the young are dark brown. These huge birds of the sea only spend time on land during the long incubation period when they hatch a single egg and then rear the fledgling.

Geographic distrubtion. Once present in large numbers throughout the islands of the Ogasawara (Bonin) to the south-east of Japan, they are now seen only on Torishima.

Habitat. The high seas.

Population. Of the one million examples existing in the nineteenth century, only a small number survives today. By 1986 there were 146 adults and 77 fledglings, and the population is growing.

JAPANESE CRESTED IBIS
Nipponia nippon

CLASS
Aves

SUBCLASS
Neornithes

ORDER
Ciconiiformes

FAMILY
Ibis

SUBFAMILY
Threskiormithinae

GENUS
Nipponia

Description. The Japanese Crested Ibis has grey and white plumage on the body and a brick-red coloured head. The legs are dark red and the long, slender, downward-curving beak is black. It generally lays two eggs.

Geographic distribution. Until 80 years ago the species was common throughout Japan; it was also found in northern China, Manchuria and Korea, where the last was seen in 1936, and then rediscovered in China in 1980 with around 40 present in 1987.

Habitat. Marshes surrounded by large groups of trees.

Population. One of the rarest birds in the world; the species was greatly reduced as a result of persecution by man between 1870 and 1890 and the deforestation carried out during and after the Second World War.

BEARDED VULTURE
Gypaetus barbatus

CLASS
Aves

SUBCLASS
Neornithes

ORDER
Falconiformes

FAMILY
Accipitridae

SUBFAMILY
Aegypiinae

GENUS
Gypaetus

Description. The Bearded Vulture is a powerful-looking bird, measuring 5ft (1.50m) from the end of its beak to the tip of its tail; it has a wingspan of more than 8½ft (2.60m) and weighs 15lb (7kg). The female is the same size as the male. There are certain characteristics which differentiate the Bearded Vulture from the true vulture species: the large head, which is covered in white feathers with a strip of black feathers running down from the top of the head, through the eye, and hanging from below the bill, like a beard; and the long wedge-shaped tail. The Bearded Vulture lives at a great height and the iron in the rocks stains the feathers and gives the bird quite a different colour from those in captivity. The Bearded Vulture usually lives in pairs. No other bird of prey can match the sharpness of its sight nor the speed of its flight, travelling as it does high over valleys and plains in search of carrion and prey. According to the area that it inhabits, the Bearded Vulture feeds off carrion of either wild animals or domestic livestock, and in particular, sheep's afterbirth. It sometimes eats tortoises, cracking the shell – using the same method for breaking bones to eat the marrow – by dropping it from a great height on to rocky ground.

Geographic distribution. Until several decades ago this species was distributed over the mountain chains of central and southern Europe; from Spain and the Balkans across all central Asia as far as northern China; and south to North and East Africa.

Habitat. Medium and high mountains.

Population. The exact population is unknown, although there are probably only a few pairs as a result of hunting by shepherds and hunters who use traps to kill it. The species was almost exterminated in Europe, but under protection is slowly recovering.

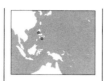

PHILIPPINE EAGLE
Pithecophaga jefferyi

CLASS
Aves

SUBCLASS
Neornithes

ORDER
Falconiformes

FAMILY
Accipitridae

SUBFAMILY
Buteoninae

GENUS
Pithecophaga

Description. The Philippine or Monkey-eating Eagle, the only representative of its genus, is a ferocious-looking bird. It has a strong head and high hooked beak that measures up to 2in (51mm) in length and 1in (21mm) wide. It was first discovered in 1894 and recalls the Old World Harpy Eagle of Central and South America. It is just under 3ft (1m) long and weighs 9lb (4kg). Its diet consists mainly of monkeys, but it will also eat domestic livestock and dogs. In captivity it easily adapts to a diet of horse meat, rabbit and poultry. Its hunting territory extends over 12sq miles (30sq km). It reproduces every two years and is believed to lay a single egg. Very rare, it was still possible to see a few examples in European and American zoos in the 1970s. The species does not live long in captivity, and by the mid 1980s only a handful survived.

Geographic distribution. Once distributed on the islands of Luzon, Samar, Leyte, and Mindanao in the Philippines. Today it is only present on Mindanao and Luzon where a small population had begun to rebuild itself.

Habitat. Dense rain forest even close to human settlement.

Population. In the late 1980s the total population was estimated at less than 200. Its decline was largely due to hunting, a mounted bird was highly prized by locals. Currently the main threat is deforestation.

SWINHOE'S PHEASANT
Lophura swinhoei

CLASS
Aves

SUBCLASS
Neornithes

ORDER
Galliformes

SUBORDER
Galli

FAMILY
Phasianidae

SUBFAMILY
Phasianiniae

GENUS
Lophura

Description. Swinhoe's Pheasant can be classified with Edwards's Pheasant and the Imperial Pheasant as part of the group of "blue pheasants," a name which is derived from the characteristic colouring of the males of these three species. Although this small group has similarities to other species of pheasant, there are marked differences in appearance and habit.
Geographic distribution. At one time the species was evenly distributed over the island of Taiwan. Now it is only found in the mountains.
Habitat. Woods on hills and mountains.
Population. Due to the very limited area that the species now inhabits and the destruction of its habitat, Swinhoe's Pheasant has become extremely rare in the wild, but abundant in captivity.

EDWARDS'S PHEASANT
Lophura edwardsi

CLASS
Aves

SUBCLASS
Neornithes

ORDER
Galliformes

SUBORDER
Galli

FAMILY
Phasianidae

SUBFAMILY
Phasianiniae

GENUS
Lophura

Description. This pheasant has a short white crest with black flecks; the rest of its plumage is a dark blue except on the wings, which are a beautiful silky green colour.
Geographic distribution. Edwards's Pheasant is confined to central Vietnam.
Habitat. Lives in thick undergrowth up to 3,280ft (1,000m).
Population. Population of Edwards's Pheasant in the wild is unknown. The species has been endangered as a result of the destruction of its natural habitat and persecution by hunters for its plumage.

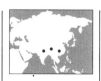

WHITE EARED-PHEASANT
Crossoptilon crossoptilon

CLASS
Aves

SUBCLASS
Neornithes

ORDER
Galliformes

FAMILY
Phasianidae

SUBFAMILY
Phasianinae

GENUS
Crossoptilon

Description. There are three species of the genus *Crossoptilon*. Those considered rare are the White Eared-pheasant with its three subspecies, *C.c. crossoptilon* (illustrated below), *C.c. drouynii*, and *C.c. harmani*. They have white plumage which is black on the nape, wings, and tail. The tip of the tail feathers is blue-green. The subspecies *harmani* has slate-coloured plumage. None of the three subspecies of the White Eared-pheasant has the tufts on the auricular region which characterize the other species of the genus, giving them the name "Eared-pheasants." These large mountain pheasants are quite similar in their habits: they are very gregarious and live together in large groups; they feed off the ground with their strong beaks. They eat tubers, roots and bulbs as well as insects and worms. The groups split up in the spring when the male chooses a territory for himself and then finds a mate.

Mating is often preceded by a form of nuptial dance in which the male courts the female, following her and swirling around her with one wing lowered. The species spends the night in trees.

Geographic distribution. The subspecies *C.c. crossoptilon* inhabits central and western Szechwan and north-eastern Yunnan. The subspecies *C.c. drouynii* inhabits the region of the upper Yangtze and Mekong in south-eastern Tibet. *C.c. harmani* inhabits the Abor and Mishmi hills in south-eastern Tibet and also northern Assam.

Habitat. Mountain forests up to the limit of tree growth, and the meadows beyond them.

Population. The populations of the species and subspecies are unknown, but it is locally common in Szechwan.

CLASS
Aves

SUBCLASS
Neornithes

ORDER
Galliformes

SUBORDER
Galli

FAMILY
Phasianidae

SUBFAMILY
Phasianinae

GENUS
Syrmaticus

ELLIOT'S PHEASANT

Syrmaticus ellioti

Description. Elliot's Pheasant (the male is illustrated below), is one of the small group of pheasants characterized by bars across the tail, giving them the name "Chequered-tailed Pheasants." Like the other species in this group, Elliot's Pheasant is also characterized by the absence of a quiff of feathers on the head, the highly developed and erectile caruncles, and by the tail which is extremely long in the male. Elliot's Pheasant is considered one of the most spectacular pheasants reared in captivity. The colouring of the male is especially brilliant, in contrast to the female's more subdued colours. It is possible to distinguish between the male and the female even when young, because of the male's alternately white and chestnut-brown striped tail feathers; the female's tail is both shorter and uniformly grey. The eggs – generally a clutch of ten – are laid towards the middle of March. The incubation period lasts 25 days; the eggs are small and pink. Elliot's Pheasant was discovered in 1872 by the naturalist Swinhoe in Zhejiang and in southern Anhui.

Geographic distribution. At one time distributed over large parts of south-east China. Today it inhabits the same area, but in greatly reduced numbers.

Habitat. The preferred habitat of the species is thick mountain forest.

Population. The population of the species in the wild is unknown but it is estimated that a very small number inhabits a few restricted regions, and it is believed that it is still in decline in the wild. The destruction of the forest and hunting have caused its decline. It is relatively common in captivity.

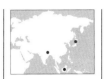

CLASS
Aves

SUBCLASS
Neornithes

ORDER
Galliformes

SUBORDER
Galli

FAMILY
Phasianidae

SUBFAMILY
Phasianinae

GENUS
Syrmaticus

MIKADO PHEASANT
Syrmaticus mikado

Description. The Mikado Pheasant is principally distinguishable from other species by the strong colouring of the male's plumage which is a beautiful blue-black, with a violet border to the feathers on the back, rump and chest, and a white border on the scapular feathers, the secondaries and their coverts. The tail is black with transverse bands of white. Hume's Pheasant, (*Syrmaticus humiae*),also belongs to the genus *Syrmaticus*. The male has a dark brown head with whitish eyebrows, a steel-coloured neck and shimmering green throat. The tail is grey, decorated with transversal stripes in black bordered by brown. The incubation period for both these species is 26 days. The Mikado Pheasant was discovered in 1906 by Goodfellow who brought it to Europe in 1912. Hume's Pheasant was not introduced into Europe until 1963.

Geographic distribution. The Mikado Pheasant is only found in the mountain area of Taiwan over a height of 6,500ft (2,000m). Hume's Pheasant is distributed over the mountains of Burma to the border of China, Tibet and India, at a height of between 6,500 - 9,800ft (2,000 - 3,000m).

Habitat. These species inhabit mountain forest rich in undergrowth.

Population. The Mikado Pheasant probably numbers no more than a few hundred. Hume's Pheasant is not thought to be in any immediate danger. Examples of both species in captivity guarantee their survival.

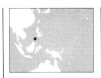

PALAWAN PEACOCK PHEASANT

Polyplectron emphanum

CLASS
Aves

SUBCLASS
Neornithes

ORDER
Galliformes

SUBORDER
Galli

FAMILY
Phasianidae

SUBFAMILY
Phasianinae

GENUS
Polyplectron

Description. The Palawan Peacock Pheasant is one of the world's most beautiful and attractive birds. The plumage on the back of the male (illustrated below) is metallic blue with shimmering green and gold highlights. The wings are a similar colour, though paler. The head is crowned with a tall, erect green quiff with blue tints. There are patches of white on the cheeks and fine white lines run above each eye, rather like eyebrows. The "eyes" on the tail and primary feathers are metallic green encircled with gold. The female is smaller with brown plumage: the quiff is generally not erect. The Palawan Peacock Pheasant was first imported to America in 1929 where it reproduced successfully in captivity. The first couple imported into Europe in 1931 came from California.

Geographic distribution. Today the species is limited to Palawan Island in the south-west Philippines where it is still widespread.

Habitat. Thick lowland and hill forest rich in undergrowth.

Population. Numbers in the wild are unknown, and although it does not appear to be in danger of extinction it is considered in a vulnerable position. Records indicate that there has been a significant decline over the last few decades which is attributed to deforestation and uncontrolled hunting. It is common in St Paul's National Park, Palawan Island. This pheasant reproduces successfully in captivity.

CLASS
Aves

SUBCLASS
Neornithes

ORDER
Gruiformes

FAMILY
Gruidae

SUBFAMILY
Gruinae

GENUS
Grus

JAPANESE OR RED-CROWNED MANCHURIAN CRANE

Grus japonensis

Description. The Japanese or Red-crowned Manchurian Crane is probably the most beautiful of all the cranes, and frequently appears in the legends, folklore, and art of Japan. Its thick white plumage contrasts with the black wing feathers; two dark stripes extend from its head and encircle the throat. The bare crown of its head is red. The long strong legs are black. The Japanese crane is one of the largest of the species, standing 4ft (1.30m) high; with wings 26 − 28in (65 − 70cm) long. The female normally lays one egg (occasionally two). Incubation lasts about 30 days and is carried out by both parents. The young are born covered in a reddish brown down. They soon leave the nest and within nine weeks are able to accompany their parents.

Geographic distribution. The Manchurian Crane once inhabited Manchuria, eastern China, Korea and Japan. It is now restricted to two small areas on the Japanese island of Hokkaido. There are also small nesting populations in China, North and South Korea, and the Soviet Union.

Habitat. The species nests in marshy terrain.

Population. The disappearance of the marshes and intensive hunting had almost brought the species to the brink of extinction by the end of the nineteenth century. Its current population is known fairly precisely: in 1985 research carried out in Japan estimated the number to be 384, in 1987 the Russians estimated their population of Manchurian Cranes was between 150 and 200. It is strictly protected in Japan where it is considered a "natural monument." By the late 1980s there were around 1,450 birds in the wild. They are present in zoos where they breed fairly successfully.

GHARIAL
Gavialis gangeticus

CLASS
Reptilia

SUBCLASS
Archosauria

ORDER
Crocodylia

SUBORDER
Eusuchia

FAMILY
Gavialidae

GENUS
Gavialis

Description. The order Crocodylia, which was rich in species in prehistoric times, can be divided into three families: Alligatoridae, Crocodilidae and Gavialidae. Many of these species are now rare and some in grave danger of extinction, principally because of hunting for their highly prized skins. Known since ancient times, the Gharial is the only living species of the family Gavialidae. This species can measure up to 23ft (7m). It has an extremely long and slender snout. Sexually mature males have a characteristic swelling on the tip of the snout. The upper jaw has 54 teeth and the lower jaw has 48; these are used for seizing and holding prey. The Gharial feeds mainly on fish. It is a dark olive colour with darker patches on the upper parts. Its flanks are shades of greenish yellow with pale underparts. The female lays the eggs directly on to the ground or on to sand banks. The young measure 16in (40cm) at birth.

Geographic distribution. The drainage basin of the Ganges and Brahmaputra in India; the Koladan and the mouth of the Maingtha in Indochina.
Habitat. It is highly aquatic: rivers and swampy estuaries.
Population. The species was sacred to the god Visnu and for a long time was not harmed by man. It then fell prey to hunters and has now been eliminated from a large part of its original range. It was also threatened by the construction of dams and canals and caught in fishermen's nets. By 1958, the exportation of almost all crocodile skins was made illegal, though hunting continued. The Gharial gained complete protection in India in 1972. A programme of captive breeding and reintroduction has been successfully implemented and the species is now recolonizing a few of its former habitats.

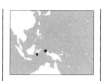

KOMODO DRAGON
Varanus komodoensis

CLASS
Reptilia

SUBCLASS
Lepidosauria

ORDER
Squamata

SUBORDER
Sauria

FAMILY
Varanidae

GENUS
Varanus

Description. The Komodo Dragon is the largest living lizard. Adults can measure more than 10ft (3m) in length, and weigh up to 310lb (140kg). This gigantic reptile has a large, heavy head, a massive body, powerful legs with sharp clawed feet, and a long tail. The skin, pitted and covered in lumps, is grey-black. The tongue is long, slender, and deeply forked. It is not surprising that the legendary descriptions of the local population and travellers were frightening accounts of this great beast. Although there had been many reports and sightings, it was only in 1912 that the Komodo Dragon was scientifically classified. Since then it has been the subject of extensive study. This large, heavy saurian is lethargic and will hide away in vegetation, making it difficult to observe; or will spend many hours lying immobile in the sun. However, once jerked into action it becomes surprisingly agile. They are able to climb trees and are good swimmers. The Komodo Dragon is basically carnivorous, feeding off medium-sized vertebrates such as wild pig and deer. It kills its prey with its powerful curved claws and sharp teeth. It is able to tear off a deer's hind limb without any apparent difficulty. They are also documented as having preyed on humans. Females lay several clutches of about 15 – 18 eggs per year.

Geographic distribution. The distribution of this reptile is not limited totally to Komodo Island. It is also found on the small islands of Rintja, Padar and Gili Moto Oewada Sami; and the western coast of the larger island of Flores. However, the species is threatened with extinction on Flores and Padar.

Habitat. The Komodo Dragon is of necessity limited to an area with a large amount of trees and accompanying vegetation, which it requires for refuge and protection. This is also the habitat of its natural prey. In some regions, such as Padar and Flores, the habitat is being transformed to such an extent that it no longer offers sufficient protection for the survival of the species.

Population. The species is protected by the Indonesian government; the islands of Rintja and Padar have been declared nature reserves. The unfavourable conditions on Padar have led the Forestry and Conservation Department to intervene with a project to re-establish the natural vegetation of the island. Illegal hunting of the species has also contributed to its decline as has competition from man in killing the Komodo Dragon's food sources.

AUSTRALASIA

PARMA WALLABY
Macropus parma

CLASS
Mammals

SUBCLASS
Metatheria

ORDER
Marsupialia

FAMILY
Macropodidae

SUBFAMILY
Macropodinae

GENUS
Macropus

Description. This small kangaroo has a beautiful brown coat with white belly, chest, and throat. A white stripe runs down each side of its face from mouth to ear, and the upper lip is white. A fine dark brown stripe descends halfway down the back. The Parma Wallaby stands about 1ft (30cm) tall.

Geographic distribution. It originally inhabited a large area in the eastern part of New South Wales, Australia. It is also found on the small island of Kawau, off New Zealand, where it was imported at the end of the last century.

Habitat. Formerly inhabited the bush and tropical forests that surrounded the edges of Lake Illawarra, close to what is now Wollongong, to the south of Sydney. The area is now totally given over to agriculture.

Population. Until 1967 it was believed that the Parma Wallaby had become extinct in 1932 on the mainland of Australia. However, in 1966 populations of wild Parma Wallabies were discovered on the Australian mainland, between the Hunter and Clarence Rivers, in New South Wales. A colony of Parmas was also discovered on the island of Kawau, remnants of those imported from Australia. These had been hunted relentlessly by the local farmers who considered them harmful to agriculture. Between 1966 and 1970, 384 specimens of the Parma were taken to various zoos where they have continued to flourish and breed successfully. The species in the wild is now protected and the park in the Gulf of Hauraki, in the most southern part of Kawau, is now a reserve.

BRIDLED NAIL-TAILED WALLABY

Onychogalea fraenata

CLASS
Mammals

SUBCLASS
Metatheria

ORDER
Marsupialia

FAMILY
Macropodidae

SUBFAMILY
Macropodinae

GENUS
Onychogalea

Description. The Bridled Nail-tailed Wallaby is distinguished from its two conspecies, Nail-tailed Wallaby (*O. unguifera*) and the Crescent-tailed Wallaby (*O. lunata*), by the two white stripes – the bridle – extending down its sides from cheek to hip. The other part of its name, Nail-tailed, derives from the horny tip on the end of its tail rather like a nail. The incisors and molars of these three species differ from other wallabies. The Nail-tailed Wallaby and Crescent Nail–tailed Wallaby have different white markings. All three are small, about the size of a hare. Their coat is thick and very soft.

Geographic distribution. The distribution of all three species is limited. The Bridled Nail-tailed Wallaby is restricted to the interior of New South Wales and southern Queensland, Australia. The Nail-tailed Wallaby, the most abundant of the three, is found in northern Australia. The Crescent Nail-tailed Wallaby is found in southern Australia and the last recorded sighting was in the 1930s.

Habitat. Forest and bushland. The Nail-tailed Wallaby prefers forests and rocky areas near rivers.

Population. The Bridled Nail-tailed Wallaby was once the most common of the three species; now it is the most rare. It was believed to have become extinct in the 1930s, but was rediscovered in 1973 near Dingo, Queensland. Part of the area where it is found is now a reserve and a captive colony has been established.

YELLOW-FOOTED ROCK WALLABY
Petrogale xanthopus

CLASS
Mammals

SUBCLASS
Metatheria

ORDER
Marsupialia

FAMILY
Macropodinae

GENUS
Petrogale

Description. The kangaroos of the genus *Petrogale* have been given the nickname "Australian chamois" because of their exceptional agility. This comes from the structure of the ball of the foot. The tail also aids balance; it is long, cylindrical and hairy with a tuft of hair on the end. When frightened, the Rock Wallaby sounds an alarm by thumping the ground.

Geographic distribution. Australia, the southern mountainous areas, north-east New South Wales and south-east Queensland.

Habitat. Rocky hills and screes.

Population. This wallaby has become rare throughout the areas of its distribution as a result of being continually hunted for its valuable pelt and from competition in its natural environment. It has been protected for many years, and several small breeding colonies are being maintained in Australian zoos.

EASTERN NATIVE CAT
Dasyurus viverrinus

CLASS
Mammals

SUBCLASS
Metatheria

ORDER
Marsupialia

FAMILY
Dasyuridae

SUBFAMILY
Dasyurinae

GENUS
Dasyurus

Description. The Eastern Native Cat can be distinguished from the others of its genus by the absence of flecks on its tail, which has a white apex; and by the fact that it has four toes, not five, on its hindfeet. The colour of its coat varies from olive-brown to almost black speckled with white flecks. Its overall length reaches 28in (70cm), 10 − 12in (25 − 30cm) of which are the tail. As with all the native cats, the Eastern Native Cat is a relentless hunter, abominated by farmers for the damage it does to henhouses. Apart from poultry and eggs, it eats wild birds, insects, snakes and lizards. It is basically nocturnal, passing the day hidden between tree roots or behind stones.

Geographic distribution. Its range covers the south-eastern part of southern Australia, the eastern half of New South Wales, east and north Victoria, King Island and Tasmania.

Habitat. The Eastern Native Cat lives principally in the eucalyptus forests with dense dry undergrowth, and in the coastal woods.

Population. The species may be extinct on the Australian continent but is still common in Tasmania. They breed regularly in zoos.

CLASS
Mammals

SUBCLASS
Metatheria

ORDER
Marsupialia

FAMILY
Dasyuridae

SUBFAMILY
Myrmecobiidae

GENUS
Myrmecobius

NUMBAT
Myrmecobius fasciatus

Description. The body and shoulders are of a beautiful brown flecked with white hairs. The back is marked with alternate black and white bands. There is a black stripe across the eye to the base of the ear; parallel to this, above and below, run two thick white stripes. Another characteristic of the coat is that the long hairs of the tail stand straight out like a bottle-brush. The male is about the size of a rat. The female is smaller and not obviously marsupial, but the area around the four nipples is covered with shaggy hair to which the young cling for the length of time they are feeding from her. The young, usually four, are born between January and May, and are carried and cared for by the mother. The Numbat has five toes on the forefeet and four on the back. There are 52 small, overcrowded, involute teeth unequally divided between the two jaws. The Numbat feeds on insects and larvae, particularly on ants and termites which it hunts, unlike most mar-supials, in the daytime. The long tongue is especially well designed for its diet and can easily penetrate cracks in trees to reach the termites.

Geographic distribution. The species was once spread out over the most southern part of north-eastern Australia and the eastern part of southern Australia, but is now restricted to a small area of western Australia.

Habitat. Bush and forest.

Population. The Numbat is now limited to a small area of western Australia, although not even an approximate figure of the population is known. Its continuing decline is due to the destruction of the forest trees which serve as protection, particularly from its more recent enemies introduced by man, such as the dog, and the wolf. They have bred in captivity in recent years and in 1988 a reintroduction programme linked with fox control was initiated.

SCALY-TAILED PHALANGER

Wyulda squamicaudata

CLASS
Mammals

SUBCLASS
Metatheria

ORDER
Marsupialia

FAMILY
Phalangeridae

SUBFAMILY
Phalangerinae

GENUS
Wyulda

Description. The Scaly-tailed Phalanger, or Possum, looks much like the other Phalangeridae, and is the size of a squirrel. It is characterized by its tail: the base is covered with dense fur but the middle and the tip are hairless and scaly; it is prehensile. The coat is short and thick, grey to grey-brown in colour. It is a solitary animal. Like most other marsupials it gives birth to one offspring at a time.

Geographic distribution. Although only a few have been captured, its range covers a wide area, with sightings in East, Central and North Kimberley, Australia.

Habitat. The species seems to spend most of the day in the sandstone areas between rocks. At night it searches for food.

Population. The first intimation of the Scaly-tailed Phalanger came from Valley Station on the outskirts of Turkey Creek, where it was sighted in 1917. It was another 25 years before the second example was sighted by the missionary J. R. B. Love on the edge of his mission at Kunmunya, 250 miles (400km) north of Derby. The Worora, natives of the area, seemed to know the animal well; they said it was common throughout their territory and was called a "llangurra." The third Possum was a female with its young captured in 1954 at Wotjulum, a mission halfway between Kunmunya and Derby. A fourth was sighted on the outskirts of Broome, south of Dampier Land. The few sightings have been attributed to the fact that the Possum seldom inhabits areas frequented by man.

BARNARD'S HAIRY-NOSED WOMBAT

Lasiorhinus barnardi

CLASS
Mammals

SUBCLASS
Metatheria

ORDER
Marsupialia

FAMILY
Vombatidae

GENUS
Lasiorhinus

Description. Barnard's Hairy-nosed Wombat is the rarest of its kind in Queensland, Australia. It is distinguished from the hairless-nosed wombats by the white and brown hair between its nostrils. Its fur is thick and soft. The species feeds exclusively off certain grasses and shoots. The incisor teeth are strong and chisel-shaped. They grow continuously and are rootless. They are enamel-coated on the front and sides. Wombats are nocturnal and excavate extensive complex burrows which are often dangerous to cattle and horsemen. They produce one, sometimes two, young. The young stay in the mother's pouch for six to seven months.

Geographic distribution. The species is found in two restricted areas in eastern Queensland, about 80 miles (130 km) north-west of Clermont, and on the coastal strip of southern Australia.

Habitat. Barnard's Hairy-nosed Wombat is found in arid, open country.

Population. Barnard's Hairy-nosed Wombat has always been very rare. The species has been rigidly protected under Australian law since 1925 and a large part of its habitat has become a national park. Little is known of this population which has been in decline with the spreading of human settlements. There have been no accurate counts but there were less than 100 burrows in the 1970s. It is often considered to be conspecific with the Northern Hairy-nosed Wombat (*L. krefftii*) which occurred further south but is now extinct. There are no examples of Barnard's Hairy-nosed Wombat in captivity, but other hairy-nosed wombats are found in zoos.

TAKAHÉ
Notornis mantelli

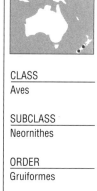

CLASS
Aves

SUBCLASS
Neornithes

ORDER
Gruiformes

FAMILY
Rallidae

SUBFAMILY
Rallinae

GENUS
Notornis

Description. This large flightless bird is the only living representative of the genus *Notornis*. There are two subspecies: *Notornis mantelli mantelli*, which was orginally found on North Island, and *N.m. hochstetteri*, found on the South Island, New Zealand. The first description of the Takahé dates from 1848 when some bone remains were discovered. The species was believed extinct until a few examples were captured and mounted for the Otago Museum in New Zealand in 1898. Following the capture of these four examples no further living trace of the Takahé was found and it was believed extinct. However, in 1948 G. B. Orbell confirmed the existence of the Takahé on South Island. It has subsequently become the symbol of the Ornithological Society of New Zealand. The bird is similar in size to a chicken; the beak and legs are reddish. The silky feathers on the chest and belly are a beautiful indigo, while the feathers on the back are shimmering green. The underside of the tail is white and the rudimentary wings are unadapted to flying. The Takahé eats seeds and shoots. The nest is built on the ground between thick vegetation. The young are born covered in a dark camouflaging down. They follow their parents to more open regions in winter.

Geographic distribution. The Takahé is now restricted to South Island, New Zealand.

Habitat. Thick forest rich in undergrowth, and humid mountain valleys c. 3,300ft (c. 1,000m).

Population. A modest increase has been recorded and it is now estimated that there are small groups of flourishing populations over an area of 200sq miles (520sq km). The decline was probably due to the alteration of habitat through climatic change, hunting by the Maoris, and the introduction of predators by the European settlers. An area of 700sq miles (1,800sq km) has been declared a protected zone and the species is no longer considered threatened.

CLASS
Aves

SUBCLASS
Neornithes

ORDER
Anseriformes

FAMILY
Anatidae

SUBFAMILY
Anatinae

GENUS
Cereopsis

CAPE BARREN GOOSE
Cereopsis novaehollandiae

Description. The Cape Barren Goose has similarities to the Common Shelduck, but differs in the shape and colouring of its beak, which is short, high, and a bright green colour; and in the colouring of its legs, which are red with black toes. This species is not gregarious, preferring to live in pairs or small groups. It lives near water, but it is basically land-living, and takes to water reluctantly. It is diurnal and feeds on grasses and young tender shoots. It occasionally emits an extraordinary squawk, similar to a pig's grunt, which has earned it the name of "Pig Goose." Reproduction takes place during the summer. The pairs isolate themselves from other individuals in the group and the female finds a suitable hollow in the ground, where she builds a nest of grasses completely lined with down. Four to six eggs are incubated for about 30 days. The goslings are able to leave the nest, following the mother in search of food, shortly after birth. The male is extremely aggressive while the female occupies the nest, and is capable of killing any intruder that comes too close. The species reproduces successfully in captivity.

Geographic distribution. Southern Australia, Tasmania, and a few islands in the Bass Straits. In 1915 four examples were introduced into New Zealand, although by 1936 it was no longer seen there.

Habitat. The Cape Barren Goose prefers areas near water where grasses and young shoots are plentiful.

Population. The species is still rather rare, although it is not considered threatened. It is commonly seen in wildfowl collections and zoos.

KAGU
Rhynochetos jabatus

CLASS	Aves
SUBCLASS	Neornithes
ORDER	Gruiformes
FAMILY	Rhynochetidae
GENUS	*Rhynochetos*

Description. The Kagu is a strange, flightless, timid bird which inhabits New Caledonia. It has a grey body with black and white wings and a long, shaggy crest. It builds its nest on the ground and the female lays three or four eggs which are incubated alternately by both parents; the eggs hatch after 35 days.

Geographic distribution. The island of New Caledonia.

Habitat. Thick forests with rich undergrowth and moist ground.

Population. Estimated at between 500 and 1,000. The prime causes of its steady decline have been the introduction on to the island of domestic predators, particularly dogs and pigs, the transformation of its natural environment, and hunting. The species is rigidly protected.

SCARLET–CHESTED PARAKEET
Neophema splendida

CLASS	Aves
SUBCLASS	Neornithes
ORDER	Psittaciformes
FAMILY	Psittacidae
SUBFAMILY	Psittacinae
GENUS	*Neophema*

Description. The Scarlet-chested Parakeet is one of the smallest, most beautiful and most brightly coloured of all parrots. It is approximately 8in (20cm) long, and has green feathers on the back, blue and black wings, a blue head, yellow belly, and scarlet chest.

Geographic distribution. The Scarlet-chested Parakeet was once distributed over a large part of southern Australia. Today, it is found only on the Eyre peninsula — apart from very occasional sightings in some regions of southern and western Australia.

Habitat. Semi-arid zones; it nests in dry tree trunks.

Population. Exact numbers unknown. The species has probably always been rare. It is protected. The species is present in various zoos and private collections where it does reproduce.

KAKAPO OR OWL PARROT

Strigops habroptilus

CLASS
Aves

SUBCLASS
Neornithes

ORDER
Psittaciformes

FAMILY
Psittacidae

SUBFAMILY
Strigopinae

GENUS
Strigops

Description. The Kakapo, or Owl Parrot, is heavily built, similar to other nocturnal birds of prey; it has short, rounded wings, a medium-length tail, long tarsi and large toes ending in very strong, curved claws. Like the owl, its large eyes are surrounded by disks of modified feathers. Its food consists of leaves, shoots, seeds, mosses, berries, fruit and other vegetation. It is an earthbound bird, occasionally climbing trees. The species reproduces only once every two years. In the mating season, the males put on a show and emit strange shrieks. The Kakapo makes its nest either in decaying tree trunks, excavating near the roots, or in a fallen tree. The bottom of the rough nest is covered with wood shavings where the female lays two to four eggs. Little is known of the habits of this bird in the wild. Attempts have been made to breed it in captivity, but with little success.

Geographic distribution. This species at one time was widely distributed across the North and South Islands of New Zealand and Chatham and Stewart Islands.
Habitat. Forest and mountains up to 6,500ft (2,000m).
Population. There is reason to believe that the numbers are still diminishing. The species has progressively disappeared as a result of the destruction of its habitat by man and the introduction on to the island of various predatory animals which have found the practically defenseless Kakapo very easy prey. The species is now legally protected. By the 1980s there were populations on Stewart Island (up to 40), Fiordland, South Island, and an introduced population on Little Barrier Island.

CLASS
Aves

SUBCLASS
Neornithes

ORDER
Psittaciformes

FAMILY
Psittacidae

SUBFAMILY
Nestorinae

GENUS
Nestor

KAKA
Nestor meridionalis

Description. According to some authorities there are three subspecies of *Nestor meridionalis*: the typical *Nestor meridionalis meridionalis*, the northern *N.m. septentrionalis*, and the third, which has been extinct since the middle of the nineteenth century, *N.m. productus*. Another species, the Kea (*Nestor notabilis*), belongs to the same genus. Primarily active at dusk, it is believed that before Europeans settled in New Zealand, the *Nestorinae* had habits similar to other parrots, eating seeds, fruits, and shoots. When the white settlers transformed and destroyed the natural habitat of the islands, as well as introducing sheep, their feeding habits changed. Instead of being purely vegetarian they quickly adapted to eating any sort of animal remains they could find — the placenta of sheep, carrion and even meat that was thrown out by slaughterhouses — as many of the plants that they had previously fed on no longer existed. They soon developed into true predators according to local sheep farmers, who reported that largish flocks would kill and eat sheep. The *Nestorinae*, like the majority of other parrots, nest in holes in trees. The Kea lays two to four eggs; the young are reared by both parents until completely self sufficient. The Kaka lays four to five eggs.

Geographic distribution. Before becoming extinct, *Nestor meridionalis productus* inhabited Norfolk and Phillip Islands, New Zealand; *N.m. septentrionalis* is found on North Island, while *N.m. meridionalis* is found on South Island and Stewart Island.

Habitat. The mountains of New Zealand up to the tree line.

Population. The birds have been persecuted by sheep rearers who consider them a serious nuisance and, in fact, a reward was paid to anyone who succeeded in killing one of them.

TUATARA
Sphenodon punctatus

CLASS
Reptilia

SUBCLASS
Lepidosauria

ORDER
Rhynchocephalia

FAMILY
Sphenodontidae

GENUS
Sphenodon

Description. The Tuatara is the oldest, sole living representative of an otherwise extinct order, a "living fossil." Its total length is 14 – 24in (36 – 61cm), and its large, strong body easily weighs over 2lb (1kg). A crest of horny tubercles runs down its back. Its large eyes with vertical pupils suit the species' nocturnal habits and it functions best between 52°F (11°C) and 55°F (13°C). It has a slow metabolism and reaches maturity only at 20 years of age. The eggs, with paper-thin shells, are laid in clutches of 8 – 15 and the young hatch after 13 – 14 months' incubation. The Tuatura's cry is a sad, tearful lament.

Geographic distribution. Originally distributed over all the New Zealand area but currently only found on some 20 islets off the New Zealand coast.

Habitat. Rocky islands with plenty of low forest or scrub cover. It usually digs underground burrows, but where it finds a subterranean nest belonging to a sea bird, such as shearwater or petrel, the Tuatara will use it, chasing out the occupants and eating the nestlings if the nest is not already abandoned.

Population. The reasons for the disappearance of this animal seem to derive more from climatic change than from deliberate harm, for the Maoris have not actively hunted the Tuatara (except to eat them occasionally), but the vegetation has altered. Domestic animals introduced on to the island have substantially interfered with the species; sheep in particular have destroyed insects, which in turn, were a food source for the Tuatara. A census carried out in 1964 estimated that there were about 10,000 individuals on some dozen islets. It now seems that the *sphenodon* population has reached a numerical constant. The species is strictly protected.

NORTH AND SOUTH AMERICA

SPECTACLED BEAR
Tremarctos ornatus

CLASS
Mammals

SUBCLASS
Eutheria

ORDER
Carnivora

SUBORDER
Fissipedia

FAMILY
Ursidae

SUBFAMILY
Tremarctinae

GENUS
Tremarctos

Description. The Spectacled Bear is the only representative of the subfamily Tremarctinae which was common in the Americas during the Ice Age . The male is larger than the female reaching 6ft (1.8m) in length and 31in (80cm) in height. It weighs 386lb (175kg). The principal characteristic that differentiates this bear from other black bears is the whitish or yellowish mask around the eyes and neck. The mask starts above the nose, goes around the eyes and some of the forehead, runs down the sides of the cheeks and meets again under the throat on the chest (illustrated below). The species can be either solitary or gregarious, but in the latter case generally only in family groups. Its diet consists mainly of leaves and fruit. Its climbing ability is specially developed for picking fruit and nuts. It occasionally eats meat and kills wild animals, cattle, or llamas, with blows from its strong legs. The gestation period is eight months after which the female produces three young. The first Spectacled Bear to be born in captivity was in Buenos Aires Zoo in 1947, and today many are successfully captive-bred.

Geographic distribution. The Spectacled Bear is sparsely distributed in the mountainous areas of western Venezuela, in Colombia, Ecuador, Peru and northern Bolivia.

Habitat. The species is moderately tolerant of variations in altitude, climate and vegetation of its habitat. Although it is typically tree-living, it is equally adaptable to relatively arid environments, moving from humid, tropical forests to dry bush, and open areas deprived of vegetation, such as the alpine prairies on both sides of the Andes, apart from the arid deserted western slopes of Peru.

Population. The total number of the species is not known. In the late 1960s it was estimated that there may have been from 800 to 2,000 in Peru, while in Venezuela it has always been more rare. It is reckoned that the numbers in Colombia and parts of Peru have recently been significantly reduced. It is still common in Ecuador where agriculture has not destroyed its environment; it has also survived in Bolivia. In all the countries where the numbers have been greatly reduced, man is to blame. This bear has been remorselessly hunted for sport, for food for the workers building the railways, for its fur – highly prized in Peru – and its fat. Moreover, much of its habitat has been taken over for agriculture. In order to preserve the species before the threat of extinction becomes a reality, hunting is prohibited in a few of the countries, for example in Peru, Bolivia, and Colombia, although it is difficult to impose the ban in remote areas. The species can be found in the national parks of Manu and Cutervo in Peru, in the Sierra de la Macarena Reserve, and in the Farallones de Cali and Perace Parks in Colombia, and the Sierra Nevada de Merida Park in Venezuela.

POLAR BEAR
Ursus maritimus

CLASS
Mammals

SUBCLASS
Eutheria

ORDER
Carnivora

SUBORDER
Fissipedia

FAMILY
Ursidae

SUBFAMILY
Ursinae

GENUS
Ursus

Description. The Polar Bear is one of the largest living carnivores. Adult males reach 8ft (2.50m) in length and weigh up to one ton, particularly in the Siberian arctic region where they have extra fat. The thick coat is almost impermeable and allows long periods of immersion in icy water. In autumn the pregnant female leaves the ice floes for a small, hilly islet where she tunnels and hollows out a chamber. This den then becomes covered by snowfalls. Within this warm protected refuge she gives birth to one, two, and very rarely three cubs which weigh 25 – 28oz (700 – 800g). Between March and April the mother emerges from her seclusion with the cubs. Male and female Polar Bears only cohabit in April, the mating season; for the remaining months of the year, while the female attends to the rearing of offspring, the male wanders alone in search of food. The cubs follow their mother on hunting trips during their first summer; not yet fully self-sufficient, they feed mainly on their mother's milk. During rearing the mother is unlikely to leave the ice floes and venture on land where wolves are a threat to her cubs. As soon as winter arrives the mother again retires to an underground chamber with the cubs, who are now the size of dogs. There they spend the coldest months and only emerge when the young have developed their second set of teeth. The young are now sufficiently large and strong to assist their mother in hunting, and rapidly learn the skills. Mother and young may separate during the second or third summer. Once independent, the cubs lead a solitary and errant life. Although the Polar Bear is a carnivore, it can adapt to a partially vegetarian diet when meat is scarce, eating lichen, berries and roots. In spring, when the coasts are free of snow and inhabited by colonies of breeding birds, Polar Bears will eat the eggs and fledglings. It will also attack larger mammals such as reindeer and musk-ox. Like many other bears, it is an expert and patient fisher, capable of lying in wait in the water for hours, ready to swipe a fish and send it flying on to the bank.

Geographic distribution. Limited to the arctic regions of the Northern Hemisphere, near the southern edge of the ice cap.

Habitat. Ice floes of the polar basin, the arctic islands, and northern shores of the most northerly land masses. The Polar Bear is an excellent swimmer and can cover great distances in water.

Population. It is very difficult to estimate even approximate numbers. The areas of distribution are not very extensive: the Polar Bear inhabits only a small part of the Arctic Ocean, the entire surface area is less than Europe, and the hostile environment has precluded extensive research. By the 1970s the population was thought to number about 20,000. It is fully protected in the Soviet Union and further protection by other countries within its range means that numbers are steadily increasing. Since 1973 a group of experts from the IUCN, from each of the countries within its range (Canada, USA, Greenland, Norway, and the Soviet Union), have frequently met to decide on international provisions for the safeguard of this species. It is illegal to hunt the Polar Bear in international waters, though Eskimos are still allowed to hunt a number by traditional methods. Hunting from the air, a sport favoured by some, is also strictly forbidden, as is hunting by any other motorized means, such as snowmobile. In short, the female and her young enjoy complete protection. Polar Bears are frequently found in zoos and reproduction in captivity has been relatively successful.

CLASS
Mammals

SUBCLASS
Eutheria

ORDER
Carnivora

SUBORDER
Fissipedia

FAMILY
Felidae

SUBFAMILY
Felinae

GENUS
Felis

OCELOT
Felis pardalis

Description. The Ocelot, also known as the American Leopard, is of modest dimensions: its overall length is 3 – 5ft (1 – 1.5m), including tail. In humid forest climates, its coat is ocher or orange, while in dry and more arid climates, it is greyish. The chest, abdomen, and inside of the paws are pale. Unlike many other felines, the Ocelot lives and hunts in pairs: generally hunting at night, they call to each other to signal their positions or that of their prey, usually small- or medium-sized, such as monkeys, rodents, forest deer, birds, reptiles, and amphibians. This species does not have a fixed mating season and copulation may occur at any time of the year. The gestation period lasts about 70 days and normally two to four cubs are born.

Geographic distribution. Its former range stretched from North Amercia (Arkansas, Louisiana, eastern and southern Texas, north-eastern Mexico) to South America (northern Argentina). It is now limited to the southern extremes of Texas and certain areas of Mexico; in South America its distribution has hardly changed.

Habitat. From humid tropical and subtropical forests to coastal forests and mangrove swamps, from marshy savannah to arid scrub.

Population. The present Ocelot population is unknown. In North America there has been a sharp decline in local populations of the subspecies. The typical South American subspecies is more numerous. During the 1960s and 1970s hundreds of thousands of skins were imported into Europe, many exported illegally from Brazil, where the ocelot is protected.

JAGUAR
Panthera onca

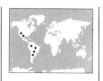

CLASS
Mammals

SUBCLASS
Eutheria

ORDER
Carnivora

SUBORDER
Fissipedia

FAMILY
Felidae

SUBFAMILY
Felinae

GENUS
Panthera

Description. Although superficially similar to the leopard, the Jaguar has a bigger build with a broader and larger head. Its tail is shorter, and the strong legs have more powerful claws. Its coat varies in colour from yellow to red-brown. The rosettes are larger and a number are decorated in the center with a small spot. It can measure up to 8½ft (2.60m), including tail. It hunts within its own territory which it marks with urine: this can vary greatly in size, across a distance of 2 – 18 miles (5 – 30km). It is mainly solitary, but during the mating season it hunts with a female. It feeds on forest mammals such as tapir, deer, monkeys, and rodents. It will also eat birds and reptiles. The gestation period lasts between 90 and 100 days; two to four cubs are born which each weigh under 2lb (1kg).

Geographic distribution. Its vast range formerly stretched from the south-west United States to Patagonia.

Habitat. An excellent swimmer, the Jaguar prefers to be near water in forest and savannah regions. It can also be found in arid areas.

Population. It is impossible to estimate numbers as its range extends over such a vast area. Some populations fairly common decades ago are now rare, if not already extinct. Among these are populations from Mexico and Arizona. The main cause of its decline - particularly during the 1960s - was the high demand for pelts for the fur trade. After 1970 this trade declined because of strict protection measures and the scarcity of the species. There are small populations in the large national parks in South America. In order to preserve the species, it must be protected within its natural habitat. Jaguars can be seen in many zoos worldwide. They reproduce fairly successfully in captivity.

MANED WOLF
Chrysocyon brachyurus

Description. The Maned Wolf is the largest and most beautiful of the numerous South American Canidae. It is 4ft 5in - 4ft 9 in (1.35 - 1.45m) long including a long tail, and measures 33in (85cm) at the shoulders. It weighs 44 - 51lb (20 - 23kg). In proportion to the body the head is small with a long muzzle. The ears are straight and have large auricles. The bright eyes are large and slanting, with an unusually meek expression for a wild carnivore. The fur is thick and soft; on the nape of the neck and back it forms a slight black mane. It is reddish brown to golden red on the back and sides, black around the mouth, nape, and limbs, and white on the throat. The tail ends in a white quiff, and is short and wide - hence the name *brachyurus*. The limbs are exceptionally long and thin which enable the Maned Wolf successfully to hunt its prey in the tall grasses of its habitat. It eats guinea pigs and other small rodents, occasionally birds, and even fruit and nuts. The broad molars are a sign of adaptation to a partly vegetarian diet. In marshy areas it also eats snails, lizards, locusts and toads. When walking it has a distinctive rolling gait, rather like a slow amble. It lifts both legs on the same side of the body at almost the same time and shifts its weight to the other side of the body. When this becomes a trot the head falls in line with the body. It is a solitary animal which seeks company only in the mating season and in order to rear its young. The gestation period is just over two months, after which two to five young are born. These weigh 1lb (500g) at birth and are covered in dark grey fur. Their lifespan is roughly the same as that of a wolf or dog. One lived to an age of more than ten years in a Washington zoo.

Geographic distribution. The interior of Brazil from the State of Piaui to Rio Grande do Sul and Mato Grosso. Extreme eastern zones of Bolivia, Paraguay and northern Argentina. Until the nineteenth century it also lived south of Rio de la Plata and in the interior of Uruguay.

Habitat. The grassland and semi-desert zones of the Chaco in Paraguay and the forest and swamps of the Mato Grosso in Brazil.

Population. The position of the Maned Wolf is vulnerable. It has always been rare and its survival in Argentina is precarious. It is, however, moderately secure in the Paraguayan Chaco and in the Mato Grosso. It is protected only in a few parks and reserves. It is extremely difficult to estimate numbers, but a study carried out in the mid 1960s estimated that there were between 1,500 and 2,200 in Brazil. The continuing destruction of their natural habitat does not bode well for this species. Both in captivity and in the wild they are susceptible to cystinuria, a hereditary disease, which often causes death. They are regularly bred in captivity.

CLASS
Mammals

SUBCLASS
Eutheria

ORDER
Carnivora

SUBORDER
Fissipedia

FAMILY
Mustelidae

SUBFAMILY
Lutrinae

GENUS
Pteronura

GIANT OTTER
Pteronura brasiliensis

Description. The Giant Otter grows to a length of 5ft (1.5m) and weighs 55lb (25kg). Gregarious by nature, this otter usually hunts for prey in a group of four to eight, but up to about 20, along the banks and in the rivers which form its habitat, usually during the day. Its diet is composed mainly of fish, but occasionally it eats small mammals, birds and their young. The Giant Otter's large body and strong teeth are immensely useful in confrontations with even fairly large predators which it fearlessly attacks. The mother gives birth to one to five young in chambers called holts, made between tree roots and vegetation along river banks. Although Giant Otters breed all year, they usually give birth during the dry season when there is no danger of the holts being flooded. This animal shows a distinct need for company which can even be satisfied by humans.

Geographic distribution. Although its population has greatly diminished, the Giant Otter is still distributed over a vast area: this includes many waterways of South America.

Habitat. Like all otters, it frequents wet environments, rivers, lakes and marshes, and is prevalent in the "black water" of the Amazon basin.

Population. It is well known that despite protection in many countries – Brazil, Peru, Ecuador and Colombia – it is still easy for fur hunters to reap a harvest of Giant Otter victims from the increasingly sparse population because of the difficulty of keeping a strict watch in such a vast area. Otter pelts have always been highly prized for their extremely soft fur, and despite protection laws, illegal trade continues.

CHINCHILLA
Chinchilla laniger

CLASS
Mammals

SUBCLASS
Eutheria

ORDER
Rodentia

SUBORDER
Caviomorpha

FAMILY
Chinchillidae

GENUS
Chinchilla

Description. The Chinchilla is halfway between a mouse and a rabbit. It measures 10in (25cm) and has a 7-in (17-cm) tail. The extreme thickness of the coat makes the fur very valuable. With 80 hairs per follicle, it is 500 times finer than human hair. Chinchillas reproduce three times a year, with one to six young in each litter.

Geographic distribution. At the time of the Spanish conquests it was common in Bolivia, Peru, Chile and the Argentine from the slopes of the Andes to the coast.

Habitat. The inaccessible and arid zones of the Andes.

Population. Hunted by the Incas, who fashioned the finest cloth from its fur, the Chinchilla was nearly exterminated between 1800 and 1900 because of the increasing value of its fur. There remain isolated colonies.

KAIBAB SQUIRREL
Sciurus aberti kaibabensis

CLASS
Mammals

SUBCLASS
Eutheria

ORDER
Rodentia

SUBORDER
Sciuromorpha

FAMILY
Sciurodea

GENUS
Sciurus

Description. The Kaibab Squirrel is roughly the same size as the North American Grey Squirrel. The Kaibab Squirrel is grizzled grey-brown, with shades of brown-red; its underside is black. The ears have long tufts of dark hair. The tail, large and thick, is white with a pale grey stripe along the top.

Geographic distribution. Exclusively inhabits the Kaibab Plateau in Colorado, USA, on the northern side of the Grand Canyon, within an area covering 30 by 70 miles (50 by 115km).

Habitat. Oak and yellow pine forest. They feed exclusively off the bark of the yellow pine.

Population. It is confined to the Kaibab National Forest and Grand Canyon National Park, and although the population has fallen to a low of 500, it is probably at carrying capacity of the habitat and range.

BLACK-FOOTED FERRET

Mustela nigripes

CLASS
Mammals

SUBCLASS
Eutheria

ORDER
Carnivora

SUBORDER
Fissipedia

FAMILY
Mustelidae

SUBFAMILY
Mustelinae

GENUS
Mustela

Description. The Black-footed Ferret is probably the rarest mammal native to the United States. Adult males are 20 – 26in (50 – 64cm) long, including tail. Most of the body is covered in a yellowish buff-coloured fur; the face, throat and belly are lighter and often almost white. It has a black mask across its face from one eye to the other. The tip of the tail and the lower parts of the legs are also black or blackish-brown. Like other mustelids, the Black-footed Ferret is equipped with anal glands which secrete a particularly offensive smelling liquid. It mainly hunts the Prairie Dog (a North American rodent distantly resembling a marmot) whose lair it usurps. The existence of the Black-footed Ferret is evidently connected to these rodents which have declined rapidly in the past 150 years.

Geographic distribution. Previously inhabited the Great Plains of North America from Canada to Texas and Arizona, and the slopes of the Rocky Mountains up to a height of 10,000ft (3,000m), the same range as the Prairie Dog. It is probably extinct in the wild.

Habitat. The Black-footed Ferret formerly inhabited prairie grassland which has largely been transformed by agriculture or been taken over for grazing.

Population. Not known, but between 1955 and the 1970s 55 confirmed sightings were made. Its numbers are probably low because of the massive poisoning campaign against the Prairie Dog which ranchers saw as dangerous competition for their cattle's grazing lands. In 1981 a colony was discovered in Wyoming and a captive breeding programme was commenced, which by 1990 was considered a success and sub-groups were being established.

CLASS
Mammals

SUBCLASS
Eutheria

ORDER
Edentata

FAMILY
Myrmecophagidae

GENUS
Myrmecophaga

GIANT ANTEATER
Myrmecophaga tridactyla

Description. The Giant Anteater, also known as the yurumi, is about the size of a large dog. Its overall length may exceed 6ft 6in (2m), including a tail of 2ft 6in (80cm). It has a very strange physical appearance. The very long head leads to an equally long, conical snout which gently curves towards the tip. There are no teeth and there is very little movement of the mandibles. The thick, strong forelegs are relatively short with powerful claws. The claw on the third digit is exceptionally long – 3in (7cm). Because of the length and shape of the claws, the Anteater walks with its fists closed, and the outer edge placed on the ground. It feeds mainly on insects, particularly ants and termites. The Anteater tears the termite mounds apart with its sharp claws and then scoops out the termites with its long, sticky tongue. The Anteater hunts at night and spends the day sleeping amongst shrubs, covered by its long bushy tail. It is a timid creature, but can defend itself by striking with its claws. The female gives birth to a single young.

Geographic distribution. Central and South America, from Southern Belize and Costa Rica to northern Argentina.

Habitat. The species lives in both the savannah and dense forest, and swamps.

Population. The population is not known, but the species has undoubtedly disappeared from areas that have been developed – as has happened in Argentina, Brazil and Peru and in particular, Central America, where it survives in places so far left untouched. The species is protected in national parks.

GIANT ARMADILLO
Priodontes maximus

Description. The Giant Armadillo is the largest of the armadillos. It can grow up to 4ft 10in (1.5m) in length including the 19-in (50-cm) tail and weighs 130lb (60kg). The upper part of the body is covered with a shell of bony plates with movable transverse bands. Owing to the flexibility of the structure and the strong cutaneous muscles, the armadillo can curl up completely; when in danger it rolls itself into a tight ball. The smooth rectangular armour plates are sparsely covered with hair. Their colour varies from yellow-beige to brown. The ears are large and rounded, and the skull heavy. The snout is larger than that of other armadillos. The hind legs are very large, with blunt claws on all five toes. The forelegs are specially adapted to digging and the digits have long curved claws; the middle digit has a massive claw - larger than that of any other animal. This claw is used to break open termite nests; the armadillo extracts the insects, its principal food, with its long cylindrical sticky tongue. When attacking the termites' stronghold the armadillo supports itself on its hind legs and muscular tail. The strong claws also provide it with an alternative means of defence. It can dig a hole in the ground with incredible speed and disappear inside it within a few seconds. The Giant Armadillo digs a hole large enough for a man to crawl into. It is a nocturnal animal, seldom entering areas inhabited by man, and only rarely crossing his path. The Brazilian natives kill the animal not so much for food but because it damages cultivated land. The name "armadillo" which is given to all the species of the Dasypodidae family, derives from the Spanish, meaning "little armed ones."

Geographic distribution. The Giant Armadillo has a very wide area of distribution – from Colombia and Venezuela to the south-east of the Andes as far as Amazonian areas of Peru and northern Argentina, including almost the whole of Brazil and the areas immediately to its west, north and south.

Habitat. The species is very rare within a vast territory. It likes the dense forest of the Amazon and the Mato Grosso, far from human population. It passes the day hidden in dens dug between huge tree roots in terrain which is not liable to flood.

Population. The species is in a vulnerable situation. Its numbers have much diminished or been wiped out in almost the whole of its territory. Apart from persecution by the natives, it is now threatened by canal and irrigation projects. The principal causes of its decline are agriculture, sheep rearing and tree felling. The opening of roads has had a serious effect in many parts of its range. It is protected in most of the countries in which it occurs, and it is found within several national parks and reserves including the Sierra de Macarena in Colombia, Manu National Park in Peru, and Mato Grosso in Brazil. If the species is to survive, it must be protected by laws in all the countries where it lives, and more of its already reduced habitat should be transformed into parks or reserves. It is rarely to be found in captivity, where it seldom survives longer than 3 – 4 years.

VICUÑA
Vicugna vicugna

CLASS
Mammals

SUBCLASS
Eutheria

ORDER
Artiodactyla

SUBORDER
Tylopoda

FAMILY
Camelidae

GENUS
Vicugna

Description. Outwardly, it is similar to the related South American Llama, Alpaca and Guanaco – some scientists classify all these species under one genus, *Llama*. The Vicuña is, however, much smaller, measuring between 28 and 30in (70 and 90cm) at the withers and usually weighing no more than 110lb (50kg). It is slim and elegant with long musclar legs, a long mobile neck, and a small head with large shining eyes and long pointed ears. The Vicuña has a unique characteristic: the lower incisors are long, narrow and grow continuously like a rodent's. This is for the constant cropping of the very short grasses of the terrain the animal inhabits. It has a long fine silky coat. The Vicuña is red-brown and whitish underneath. A white mane up to 14in (35cm) long covers the base of the throat and chest. Vicuñas live in small herds composed of between five and ten females with their young under the leadership of one male. When danger arises, the male raises the alarm with a high-pitched cry, rather like a whistle, and places himself between the danger and the fleeing females. Like the Llama, the Vicuña defends itself by spitting rapidly and hard, expelling air and saliva. It is perhaps the most graceful of the hoofed animals. It grazes on tufts of short grass; it also eats mallow leaves in sandy regions. One offspring (very occasionally two) is born, usually in February or March, after an 11 month gestation period. The young is able to stand up and move within 15 minutes of birth; it is suckled for six months and remains with the mother until nearly a year old. They usually live up to 20 years, but in captivity can reach 24. It is possible to crossbreed the Vicuña with the Llama, Alpaca and Guanaco, producing fertile hybrids. It has been crossed with the Alpaca in particular, giving what is know as the "Paco-Vicuña," a cross which is prized for the quality of its wool.

Geographic distribution. The species was one distributed over a large area in the high Andes between 10,000 and 17,000ft (3,000 and 5,000m) in Chile, Argentina, Bolivia, Peru, and Ecuador. The species is now extinct in Ecuador.

Habitat. The high plains of the Andes. In summer it prefers the zone immediately below the snow line, feeding off the succulent vegetation. During the other seasons it frequents the "puna", the high, cold arid plateau.

Population. The Vicuña's fleece was recognized by the Incas as of extremely high quality and its protection rigorously enforced. They were not hunted, but periodically rounded up and sheared. The cloth manufactured from their wool was reserved for the Inca ruling classes. After the Spanish conquest the slaughter commenced and at times as many as 80,000 a year were being killed. Although Simon Bolivar introduced protection in 1825 they continued to be persecuted until the 1970s. From 1950 to the late 1960s the population dropped from some 400,000 to perhaps below 20,000. Under an international agreement between the countries in which it occurs their numbers have rapidly rebuilt and by the mid 1980s not only had translocations taken place, but wool was once more being harvested.

CLASS
Mammals

SUBCLASS
Eutheria

ORDER
Insectivora

FAMILY
Solenodontidae

GENUS
Solenodon

CUBAN SOLENODON
Solenodon cubanus

Description. In general appearance this animal is similar to a shrew, though with a larger and less graceful body. It is 18 – 23in (45 – 58cm) in length, between a third and a fifth of which is taken up by the tail. The coat is brownish, with lighter shades on the head and belly. The Solenodon's main characteristic is the long conical snout. Its paws are large with well-developed nails. When the Solenodon bites its prey, the salivary glands beneath the jaw secrete a poison to the space all round the base of the second lower incisor; from there a channel carries the poison into the wound. It eats invertebrates and small vertebrates, such as reptiles (snakes and lizards). It is basically nocturnal, hiding in holes in trees and rocks. It moves in fits and starts, continually changing direction. It can have two litters a year, but only one or two, or exceptionally three, young are born at a time.

Habitat. Mountain forests and thickets; plantations.

Geographic distribution. While its one relative, *Solenodon paradoxus*, is limited to Hispaniola, the Cuban Solenodon is found only in Cuba, only in the eastern regions.

Population. The Solenodontidae are now limited to the above islands. Presumably the Solenodon's decline has resulted from the destruction of the woodland and the introduction of the mongoose, as well as domestic carnivores. The species is protected by law and is present in the Jaquani Reserve near Toa Baracoa. Although they have been kept in captivity, and are long-lived (one lived more than 11 years), there are no self-sustaining populations.

MOUNTAIN TAPIR

Tapirus pinchaque

CLASS
Mammals

SUBCLASS
Eutheria

ORDER
Perissodactyla

SUBORDER
Ceratomorpha

FAMILY
Tapiridae

GENUS
Tapirus

Description. There are four species of tapir, three in Central and South America and one in Asia. Although all four are in danger of extinction, the most serious threat is to the Mountain Tapir or Woolly Tapir (illustrated below). This species is smaller than the others: its maximum length is 6ft (1.80m) and it weighs no more than 550lb (250kg). The coat, characteristic only of this species, is soft and woolly, particularly on the belly. Baird's Tapir (*Tapirus bairdii*) (the largest of the American tapirs) is also thought by the IUCN to be near extinction. It grows to a length of 7ft (2.20m) and can weigh over 660lb (300kg). The tapir's diet consists of fruit, grasses and plant shoots, which are wrenched off with its long, flexible snout. This also has a tactile function as the tip is covered with sensory hairs.

Geographic distribution. The Mountain Tapir is found only in the Andes in an area covering Venezuela, Ecuador, Colombia and Peru. Baird's Tapir is found from Vera Cruz in southern Mexico, across the central American countries as far as the Colombian and Ecuadorian Andes.

Habitat. The Mountain Tapir inhabits mountain areas up to the snow line, c. 14,800ft (c. 4,500m), but it prefers the region between 6,500 and 11,500ft (2,000 and 3,500m) with its shrubby and low tree-covered vegetation. Baird's Tapir inhabits humid, tree-covered forest and low-lying swamps, although it also inhabits mountain shrubland up to 10,000ft (3,000m).

Population. The total population of the Mountain Tapir is not known. It is estimated that there are between 200 − 300 in Peru and only a few dozen in the eastern areas of Cordigliera in the Andes. Between 1966 and 1970 a considerable number were captured with high mortality and sold to zoos. Bairds's Tapir's population is unknown. Both species are now legally protected in their range.

GOLDEN LION MARMOSET
Leontopithecus rosalia

CLASS
Mammals

SUBCLASS
Eutheria

ORDER
Primates

FAMILY
Callitricidae

GENUS
Leontopithecus

Description. The Golden Lion Marmoset measures 21 – 29in (53 – 73cm), over half of which is the tail. The long silky coat is golden with a ruff of longer hair around the neck, rather like a lion's mane. The face is brownish black. In other species the coat is black with gold markings. The hand is prehensile, but the tail – in common with other members of this family – is not. They live in small groups. It is not unusual for two young to be born; they are suckled for three months and reach full size at one year. Some authorities consider the three species, R. rosalia, L. chrysomelas and L. chrysopygus, to be three well-marked subspecies.

Geographic distribution. Formerly inhabited the coastal forests of south-east Brazil. It is now confined to an area of forest measuring 350sq miles (900sq km) in the state of Rio de Janeiro.

Habitat. Tropical forest with a wide variety of flora: *Tapira guianensis*, one of its basic foods, is present through its range.

Population. In 1968 the number of Golden Lion Marmosets in the wild was estimated at 600: by 1971 numbers had dropped to 400. Their natural habitat has gradually been destroyed by the transformation of the forest for agriculture and urban settlement, as Rio de Janeiro sprawls out further and further. By 1980 the population was under 100, but a successful captive breeding programme enabled the first reintroductions to take place in 1984. By the late 1980s the world population was around 500.

RED UAKARI
Cacajao rubicundus

CLASS
Mammals

SUBCLASS
Eutheria

ORDER
Primates

SUBORDER
Simiae

FAMILY
Cebidae

SUBFAMILY
Pitheciinae

GENUS
Cacajao (uakaris)

Description. The Uakari has an overall length of 23 – 26in (59 – 67cm), with a tail 6 – 7in (16 – 19cm) long. It is characterized by a yellow coat of thick, long, coarse hair and by its brilliant crimson-red face. Little is known of the species' habits and social behaviour. It is believed to live in small groups. They move on four legs rather than two. The hand is prehensile. Although the Uakari was thought to be lazy and apathetic, it has recently been seen – at least in captivity – to be very active.

Geographic distribution. As recently as 1930 the Red Uakari lived throughout an area extending from the Amazon and Rio Yavari in eastern Peru to the south-east of Brazil. Now it ranges from the Amazon to Putumayo, in a small area of Brazil and eastern Peru. It is confined to the low altitude areas – 984ft (300m) – along the banks of the Rio Putumayo, Rio Napo and the lower reaches of Rio Ucayali, and also along the Rio Madre de Dios.

Habitat. The Uakari, a forest animal, is restricted to the bands of the Amazon forest that are periodically flooded along the river banks.

Population. The species remains rare throughout its given area. Dependency on a particular habitat restricts any migration and prevents interchange between different populations, thus endangering the species. With the destruction of their natural habitat and being unable to transfer to another area, the groups seem bound to perish. The most serious threat comes from hunting; despite being illegal, it is carried on clandestinely by professional hunters and local settlers. They are listed on Appendix I of the Convention on International Trade in Endangered Species of Wild Fauna and Flora, and banned from international trade. There are small numbers in captivity, but they breed regularly.

WOOLLY SPIDER MONKEY

Brachyteles arachnoides

CLASS
Mammals

SUBCLASS
Eutheria

ORDER
Primates

SUBORDER
Simiae

FAMILY
Cebidae

SUBFAMILY
Atelinae

GENUS
Brachyteles

Description. One of the rarest American primates, the Woolly Spider Monkey measures 43 − 45in (110 − 137cm) in length, including a 26 − 31-in (65 − 80-cm) tail. It has strong limbs with a prehensile tail which is naked near the tip. The fur is grey or brownish, with yellow or reddish shades in the male. The face is pink when young, which gradually becomes dusky in adulthood. The hands lack thumbs. The Woolly Spider Monkey moves along branches using all its four limbs. Its tail serves as an extra hand. They live high in the trees of the tropical rain forests rarely descending to the ground. They eat leaves and fruit. Little is known about this species.

Geographic distribution. It is restricted to Brazil, where it occurs in Atlantic forests of altitudes of up to 4,900ft (1,500m).

Habitat. Tropical coastal forest and mountainous rain forest.

Population. The original population is estimated at 400,000 but had fallen to under 1,000 by the beginning of the 1980s. The species is in a critical situation because of the continuing destruction of its habitat for human settlement and agriculture. It is protected and there is a ban on international trade. The largest population occurs in the Serra da Bocaina National Park; there are smaller groups in the parks of Itatiaia (Rio de Janeiro), Serra dos Orgaos (São Paulo), Rio Doce (Minas Gerais), and in the Nova Lombardia Reserve (Espirito Santo), Brazil.

GALAPAGOS LAND IGUANA
Conolophus subcristatus

CLASS
Reptilia

SUBCLASS
Lepidosauria

ORDER
Squamata

SUBORDER
Sauria

FAMILY
Iguanidae

GENUS
Conolophus

Description. A quiet, inoffensive creature, the Land Iguana has a squat, heavy body with a bulky trunk, strong limbs, cylindrical tail and a crest along its back which stands up at the neck. It also has folds of skin forming a pouch under the throat. The total length is 43in (110cm) including a 22-in (55-cm) tail. It is vegetarian. During the mating season the males fight ritual battles. The female lays her eggs in a hole which she has dug in the ground and covers them with earth.

Geographic distribution. The species is exclusive to the Galapagos archipelago.

Habitat. Terrain with sparse bush vegetation. The destruction of this has left the young of the Land Iguana undefended from the attack of buzzards.

Population. Extinct in a number of the Galapagos islands, the species is very rare in others. Indiscriminate hunting by man and persecution by indigenous birds of prey, together with the introduction of domestic animals have all been responsible for the fall in numbers of this species.

GOLDEN FROG
Atelopus zeteki

CLASS
Amphibia

SUBCLASS
Anuromorpha

ORDER
Anurans

SUBORDER
Procoela

FAMILY
Atelopodidae

GENUS
Atelopus

Description. This little frog received its name from its splendid golden colouring. It has three large, black patches across the back and dark blotches on the legs. The Golden Frog is similar to the Tree Frog but the long slim legs give it a more slender appearance. The first two toes on the feet are atrophied. The females are attracted by the mating cry of the male. They lay their eggs in rain puddles where, because of danger of evaporation, they have become adapted to develop extremely quickly, hatching out after only 24 hours.

Geographic distribution. The Anton Valley in the Central American republic of Panama.

Habitat. A territory only 1.2 miles (3km) in diameter completely surrounded by mountains, except where the River Anton flows out of the valley.

Population. Having been continually sought as souvenirs for many tourists that visit the Anton Valley, the species has apparently become rather scarce.

GALAPAGOS GIANT TORTOISE
Testudo elephantopus

CLASS
Reptilia

SUBCLASS
Anapsida

ORDER
Chelonia

SUBORDER
Cryptodira

FAMILY
Testudinidae

GENUS
Testudo

Description. The gigantic Galapagos Tortoise measures 3½ft (110cm) across its highly domed carapace. It weighs 330 – 440lb (150 – 200kg). It has massive legs protected by bone-cored scales. In various subspecies (the Saddlebacked Tortoises) the anterior part is raised allowing a fuller extension of the long neck so that it can reach higher branches. This tortoise is a good example of how various subspecies adapt to different environments. The Galapagos Giant Tortoise was described by Darwin in The Voyage of the Beagle and his observations are still highly valuable today. Because of the scarcity of water in the warm arid plains where the species lives, it has been forced to adapt its behaviour. It has developed a pattern whereby it periodically journeys up from the sea to the volcanic highlands where there are a large number of pools. There they drink, bathe, and feed off the rich vegetation. The journeys back and forth are always along the same routes and over the centuries distinct paths have been carved out of the landscape. This behaviour has become so instinctive that the Galapagos Giant Tortoise would follow the same pattern even in a different environment. There are numerous subspecies, most of which had large populations. However, most of the facts and descriptions come from historical accounts and sailors' stories. Of the 15 known subspecies, four have been extinct for some time. *T.e. abingdoni* was also thought to be extinct but in 1972 traces of two or three were discovered. The ten surviving subspecies are: *T.e. elephantopus*, which is the typical subspecies, *T.e. becki*, *T.e. chathamensis*, *T.e. darwini*, *T.e. ephippium*, *T.e. güntheri*, *T.e. hoodensis*, *T.e. microphyes*, *T.e. nigrita*, and *T.e. vandenburghi*.

Geographic distribution. The Galapagos archipelago; of the living subspecies, five are found in Albermarle, and a different one on each of the islands of James, Indefatigable, Duncan, Hood, Chatham, and Abingdon. The subspecies that are now considered extinct used to inhabit the islands of Narborough and Jervis. It is worth noting that the only other surviving group of Giant Tortoises also lives on islands in the Seychelles archipelago. While species and subspecies which inhabit islands are generally smaller than relatives found on mainland, the Galapagos Giant Tortoise and the Seychelles Giant Tortoise prove the exceptions.

Habitat. The Galapagos Giant Tortoise prefers dry land with volcanic highlands with abundant water and vegetation.

Population. All of the subspecies are rare; a few are believed to be in immediate danger of extinction. Recent sightings and recordings vary enormously for the different subspecies; from one to one thousand (*T.e. porteri*). The species has declined from the enormous numbers mentioned by the first explorers to the present state of near-extinction. This has principally been caused by the slaughter carried out by sailors over the centuries visiting the "Tortoise islands" (Galapagos is the Spanish for tortoise). These crews butchered them for their meat. The colonization of the islands and the introduction of domestic animals, particularly goats and pigs, further jeopardized the survival of large numbers. The species was protected and in 1959 the government of Ecuador declared all uninhabited areas in the Galapagos to be a national park. The Charles Darwin Station has taken steps towards ensuring the survival and increase of the species and several subspecies are being bred in capitivity.

GALAPAGOS PENGUIN

Spheniscus mendiculus

CLASS
Aves

SUBCLASS
Neornithes

ORDER
Sphenisciformes

FAMILY
Spheniscidae

GENUS
Spheniscus

Description. The Galapagos Penguin measures only 21in (53cm) in length and weighs around 5lb (2.2kg). The featherless wings are adapted to swimming and measure 9in (23cm). It is the customary black and white colour of penguins with shades of midnight blue. The Galapagos Penguin lays two white eggs which hatch after 40 days.
Geographic distribution. Limited to Fernandina and Isabella Islands in the Galapagos archipelago.
Habitat. This is the only species of penguin to live in an equatorial zone along the coasts of the Galapagos Islands where it nests in volcanic caves near the sea.
Population. The species has been reduced to a few thousand, and Galapagos Penguins are now protected.

GALAPAGOS FLIGHTLESS CORMORANT

Nannopterum harrisi

CLASS
Aves

SUBCLASS
Neornithes

ORDER
Pelacaniformes

FAMILY
Phalacrocoracidae

GENUS
Nannopterum

Description. This is the only species of cormorant unable to fly; it is also the rarest. It is about 3ft (1m) long with very small wings measuring 10in (25cm); it weighs about 4lb (2kg). It lays one or two eggs in nests made out of algae and twigs built on rocks near the sea. The incubation period is 23 – 25 days.
Geographic distribution. Limited to Isabella Island in the Galapagos Islands.
Habitat. Rocky coast.
Population. The species has fallen an easy prey to hunters because it is flightless. After a population crash in 1982 – 1983, its numbers recovered to 800 – 1,000 by 1986.

IVORY-BILLED WOODPECKER
Campephilus principalis

CLASS
Aves

SUBCLASS
Neornithes

ORDER
Piciformes

FAMILY
Picidae

SUBFAMILY
Picinae

GENUS
Campephilus

Description. This beautiful woodpecker is almost certainly extinct. With a length of 20in (50cm), the Ivory-billed Woodpecker is one of the largest members of the family Picidae, and is only exceeded by the related and equally rare Imperial Woodpecker which measures up to 22 in (55cm). The glossy black plumage has two striking white stripes on the back and neck; the wings are also black and white, and the legs are grey. The strong beak is chisel-shaped. The male (illustrated right) has a high, pointed crest of red feathers; the female, which is the same size and colour, has a black crest which is more curved. As the name indicates, the beak is ivory-white in both sexes. The female lays between one and four eggs in a hole which has been dug out of a tree trunk. They eat insects and larvae extracted from the bark and wood of trees with their long beak.

Geographic distribution. The Ivory-billed Woodpecker was once distributed throughout the southern and western United States. The Imperial Woodpecker inhabits the Sierra Madre Mountains in Mexico.

Habitat. The most impenetrable parts of dense forest and marshy territory where there is an abundance of dead and decaying trees. The Imperial Woodpecker inhabits high mountain regions.

Population. The Ivory-billed Woodpecker was always rare and, as its habitat is almost impenetrable, its existence was for a long time known only by the Indians and a few naturalists. It was highly prized by collectors because of its rarity. The major cause of its extinction was the destruction of its habitat for timber. As the forests have disappeared, so have the woodpeckers. It was already thought to be extinct in 1925, but between 1930 and 1940 a few were discovered in Louisiana and South Carolina. Since then there have been unconfirmed sightings.

CLASS
Aves

SUBCLASS
Neornithes

ORDER
Falconiformes

FAMILY
Cathartidae

GENUS
Gymnogyps

CALIFORNIA CONDOR
Gymnogyps californianus

Description. The California Condor is one of the rarest birds in the world. Its fossil remains indicate that the species existed in America as long as 200,000 years ago; some scientists believe that it had at that point reached its final stage of evolution and that now it is really a prehistoric relic which will become extinct with or without the intervention of man. No one can say whether or not this vast bird of prey will survive, but it is in a serious and precarious situation and has become symbolic of the conservationist movement in California. Its wingspan of 9½ft (2.90m) and weight of over 25lb (11kg) makes it one of the largest North American birds. It is similar in appearance and size to the more common and also more widespread Andean Condor (*Vultur gryphus*). The California Condor has a dark plumage with large white triangles underneath the wings. It has a black collar and a bald reddish head and neck. The powerful beak is a greyish yellow. The condor can glide effortlessly through the air for hours on end. It does not have the maneuverability and speed of the smaller birds of prey, but it is undoubtedly the patriarch of the skies. The species nests in high, rocky crags without using twigs or leaves, so that the single egg is laid on bare ground. The reproductive process is incredibly slow and the rate of success is very low. The egg is incubated for about 50 days and the young is reared by the parents for almost two years. Each pair therefore nests only once every two years. It takes six years for the young to develop adult plumage, but it does not reach sexual maturity until it is at least ten years old. Many eggs are lost, either rolling out of the nest when their parents' attention has been distracted; or else a frightened parent might flee from the nest, inadvertently clutching the incubating egg between its talons. Therefore, the number of young that survive each year is extremely small. If the California Condor does survive, it will be due to its resistance to the extreme conditions of its habitat, where the temperature ranges from 32°F (0°C) to 104°F (40°C), and also to its longevity: some condors in captivity have lived for almost 50 years.

Geographic distribution. During the nineteenth century the California Condor was distributed over a large part of western North America; British Columbia (Canada), Oregon, the state of Washington, and the northern part of the Mexican peninsula. By the 1970s it was limited to the southern coastal areas of the state of California between Monterey and Los Angeles, becoming extinct in the wild in 1987.

Habitat. The mountain chains along the west coast of the United States.

Population. The main reasons for the species' decline are hunting, which began in the gold rush when pioneers collected the condor's long black feathers, the disturbance of their natural habitat by tourists, air traffic, and the use of pesticides. When the last wild condor was collected in 1987 there were 26 others in captivity, from which it is hoped to rebuild the population.

BALD EAGLE
Haliaeetus leucocephalus

Description. The Great Seal of the United States of America bears a powerful imposing figure — a large eagle with a white head and white tail. This, the Bald Eagle, is related to the Eurasian eagle, the White-tailed Eagle (*Haliaeetus albicilla*) and is often associated with aquatic habitats. The head, upper part of the neck and tail of the adult Bald Eagle are covered in pure white feathers which contrast with the deep brown body, making this one of the most beautiful birds of prey. The length of body varies from 27 – 35in (70 – 90cm), with a wingspan of 6ft (188 – 197cm) in the male and over 6½ft (210cm) in the female. The adult male weighs about 9lb (4kg) and the female about 13lb (6kg). The beak is yellow and strongly hooked and the cere and legs are pale yellow. The species is more slender and agile than the White-tailed Eagle and has a rounded tail. The Bald Eagle mates for life and constructs its very large nest near the water in high pine or mangrove trees, or high up among rocks. The male and female build the nest together. Two whitish eggs are laid and incubated by both parents for 35 days. The young are born covered in grey down and develop their feathers after two months; only after three months do they venture from the nest. Even after they have learnt to fly, they will return to the nest in the evening. When the young become independent they leave their parents, often flying far away from the sea and lakes. After a few years they return to their birthplace to build their first nest and settle down. There are two geographically defined subspecies of the Bald Eagle: the northern strain (*Haliaeetus leucocephalus alascanus*), which is still fairly common, and the southern Bald Eagle (*Haliaeetus leucocephalus leucocephalus*), which is much rarer and slightly smaller.

Geographic distribution. All North America, the Bermudas, and formerly the Commander Isles off north-eastern Siberia. The southern subspecies inhabits all the southern United States and is most numerous in Florida.

Habitat. The Bald Eagle inhabits sea coasts and the banks of lakes and rivers. It watches over its territory by perching on high trees or rocks, or circling over the water in order to pick up its prey. It feeds on small mammals — rabbits and racoons for instance — aquatic birds, fish, reptiles, amphibians and even tortoises.

Population. The main cause of the dramatic decline in numbers was pollution which either killed the bird or reduced its fertility. The rate of successful clutches declined to 44 per cent. The growth of human settlement around its nesting areas has also added to its decline. The total population of the Bald Eagle can be placed in the order of tens of thousands (between 30,000 and 55,000 in Alaska, but between 3,000 and 4,000 in the other states and a number in Canada). The southern strain has a current population of between 1,000 and 1,100. The species is now protected by law throughout its range, although a few are still killed by farmers.

CLASS
Aves

SUBCLASS
Neornithes

ORDER
Gruiformes

FAMILY
Gruidae

SUBFAMILY
Gruinae

GENUS
Grus

WHOOPING CRANE
Grus americana

Description. The Whooping Crane is one of the rarest birds in North America. It is very beautiful with white plumage apart from the black wing tips. The top of the head is bare and red, with sparse, hair-like feathers. The areas between the eyes, beak, and cheeks are crimson and there is a bright pink patch on the throat. The long legs are black. The Whooping Crane is the tallest bird in North America, standing 4ft (125cm) tall. The species takes its name from its loud cry which can be heard as far as 3 miles (5km) away. It nests in Canada and winters in southern Texas where in early January the nuptial dances take place. In spring and autumn the birds migrate about 1,900 miles (3,000km) in single file. Nests are built on grass between reeds. The female lays two eggs which are incubated for about 35 days; generally only one young reaches maturity. Whooping Cranes are omnivorous and will eat any variety of food from roots to small reptiles, although their preferred food is crustaceans which they kill with a blow from the beak. The Sandhill Crane (*Grus canadensis*) is related to the Whooping Crane, and is also rare. It is similar in appearance but smaller, measuring 3½ft (110cm) in height, with grey plumage on the head and a white throat. The crimson colour is limited to the bare top of its head. It has five subspecies. The Sandhill Crane's diet consists principally of insects.

Geographic distribution. Until the middle of the nineteenth century the Whooping Crane nested throughout a large part of Canada in the provinces of Alberta, Saskatchewan, and Manitoba; in the USA, in Illinois, Minnesota, Iowa, North and South Dakota, and possibly in Montana and Nebraska. The species wintered on the coast of the Gulf of Mexico. One small population did not migrate but nested in Louisiana. Today, the species nests only in the Wood Buffalo National Park, in the southern part of the Mackenzie district in Canada, and winters in the Aransas National Reserve, Texas. The Sandhill Crane is distributed from the extreme north-east of Siberia across Alaska, Canada, a large part of central-western United States as far as California, Texas, and Florida. One subspecies, *G.c. nesiotes*, lives on Cuba.

Habitat. The Whooping Crane inhabits small marshy islands on the many lakes throughout its range. The Sandhill Crane is found in a similar habitat but it lays its eggs close to shallow water.

Population. Between 1860 and 1870 there must have been 1,300 − 1,400 Whooping Cranes. Since then numbers have declined steadily. This has been caused by hunting, particularly when the birds are in flight, and by their increasing difficulty in finding open spaces far from human settlement. Between 1933 and 1942, numbers decreased to less than 30. A low was reached in the winter of 1951-52 when only 21 birds survived. Since then, under strict protection, numbers have very slowly rebuilt; by the early 1980s over 70 wild birds survived and these were being reinforced by captive bred birds. Eggs were being placed under Sandhill Cranes to produce new flocks. Although it will be many years before the future of the Whooping Crane can be deemed safe, provided current trends continue, it will probably be considered out of immediate danger by the end of the century.

HAWAIIAN GOOSE
Branta sandvicensis

CLASS
Aves

SUBCLASS
Neornithes

ORDER
Anseriformes

FAMILY
Anatidae

SUBFAMILY
Anserinae

GENUS
Branta

Description. The Hawaiian Goose belongs to the genus *Branta* (Sea Geese) and differs from the genus *Anser* (Field Geese) in the structure of the beak, which is short, black and without the horny covering on the upper half. The Hawaiian Goose is 24 - 28in (60 - 70cm) long; the wings are about 15in (37cm) long. Its plumage is brown, black, grey, and white, and the head is covered with black feathers in the shape of a hood. The beak, legs and webbed feet are also black. This species inhabits the slopes of volcanic mountains between 4,920 and 8,200ft (1,500 and 2,500m) — an inhospitable inaccessible territory, almost always surrounded by mist, and subject to frequent rain and thunderstorms. There are no meadows, only dry lava fields which are deeply furrowed by cracks where the old lava is disintegrating, and there are a few patches of grass and bushes, and pools with shallow water. This is the refuge of the Hawaiian Goose. Over the centuries, these geese, which the locals call Ne-ne, have adapted to living in such conditions: they now live almost exclusively on land and have developed very long legs and strong toes linked by a much-reduced web. The female lays four to six eggs in hollows protected by shrubs. Their diet consists mainly of grasses and berries.

Geographic distribution. The Hawaiian Islands; on the slopes of the volcano Mauna Kea; the volcanoes Mauna Loa and Hualalei. In 1962, they were reintroduced to Haleakala Crater on the island of Maui where it was extinct.

Habitat. Semi-arid slopes of volcanoes, with sparse grass and shrubs, between 4,900 and 8,200ft (1,500 and 2,500m).

Population. The Hawaiian Goose is an example of a species which was reduced to the point of extinction but has been saved by man through captivity and reintroduction to its original territory. The species lived peacefully on the islands when they were inhabited only by the Polynesians, who hunted the geese without endangering their population. When the white man arrived on the islands of Hawaii and Maui, there were an estimated 25,000 geese. However, as happened to most of the original fauna of Hawaii, the geese were intensively hunted. White man also introduced mammals and destroyed the local habitat to rear domestic livestock. By 1950 there were less than 50 geese left, all on Hawaii Island. Although a number lived and reproduced in various zoos throughout the world, there were none in captivity after 1940. In 1950, one male and two females were captured and taken in by the Wildfowl Trust at Slimbridge in Great Britain, headed by the late Sir Peter Scott. The first nine goslings were born at Slimbridge in 1951. Meanwhile the Department of Agriculture of Hawaii had set up another reproduction center at Pohakuloa. By the 1970s the total population of the Hawaiian Goose had increased to over 1,000, and it is now considered out of danger. It is no longer necessary to transfer any geese from the Wildfowl Trust because the United States Wildlife Service has now reproduced a sufficient number for itself.

TRUMPETER SWAN
Cygnus buccinator

CLASS
Aves

SUBCLASS
Neornithes

ORDER
Anseriformes

FAMILY
Anatidae

SUBFAMILY
Anserinae

GENUS
Cygnus

Description. One of the heaviest flying birds, it is 5½ft (1.65cm) in length; the wings are 28in (69cm) long and the wingspan 10ft (3m). It weighs 30lb (13.5kg). The Trumpeter Swan is also distinguishable by the thin reddish stripe along the edge of the lower part of its black beak. The Trumpeter Swan feeds off both floating and submerged aquatic plants: it is able to obtain plants underwater by submerging its long neck. In winter the Trumpeter Swan flies to the southern parts of its range in search of mild weather and food. It reaches adulthood at three years and will then mate for life. Their nest is made of grasses and twigs and is built on top of a mound of earth, frequently on top of a Muskrat lodge. Five or six eggs are laid and incubated by the mother; the male guards the nest. The cygnets hatch out after 35 – 40 days and are reared by both parents; the mortality rate is quite high due to parasitical diseases, cygnets being crushed by their parents and, surprisingly, drowning.

Geographic distribution. North America; at one time extensive, but now limited to Alaska, Idaho, Montana, Wyoming, Alberta, and British Columbia.

Habitat. Fresh inland water: lakes, marshes, and rivers.

Population. From the 1930s numbers had declined rapidly. The primary causes were hunting for its meat and feathers. A protection system was effected by the USA and Canada, and reserves established (including Red Rock Lake near Yellowstone National Park). These measures saved the species from extinction and it is now recovering and spreading back to many of its former haunts. They are also found in a few zoos and regularly breed.

CLASS
Aves

SUBCLASS
Neornithes

ORDER
Galliformes

SUBORDER
Galli

FAMILY
Phasianidae

SUBFAMILY
Tetraoninae

GENUS
Tympanuchus

PRAIRIE CHICKEN
Tympanuchus cupido

Description. The Prairie Chicken is characterized by two tufts of slim feathers at either side of the head. These grow above two bare reddish, fleshy areas which are air sacs. The tail is very short and round. The species lives on shoots, seeds, and some insects (mainly grasshoppers). In spring the female lays 12 eggs which hatch after 23 - 24 days.

Geographic distribution. The two subspecies principally in danger are Attwater's Prairie Chicken (T.c. *attwateri*) and the Greater Prairie Chicken (T.c. *pinnatus*). The former is found in south-eastern Texas and the latter in central-southern Canada, as far as north-east Oklahoma, and as far as the Missouri in the east. The typical subspecies, known as the Heath Hen (T.c. *cupido*), has been extinct since 1932.

Habitat. The open prairies of southern Canada and the central regions of the United States.

Population. Attwater's Prairie Chicken is not numerous, but its numbers are probably as great as its habitat can support. The Greater Prairie Chicken is more widespread and abundant.

THE OCEANS

BLUE WHALE
Balaenoptera musculus

CLASS
Mammals

SUBCLASS
Eutheria

ORDER
Cetacea

SUBORDER
Mysticeti

FAMILY
Balaenopteridae

GENUS
Balaenoptera

Description. The Blue Whale is the largest animal on earth. It is larger than 30 elephants and heavier than 2,000 men. This whale (illustrated with Killer Whales) can measure 100ft (30m) in length and weigh 150 tons. It has the characteristic longitudinal furrows extending from throat to belly which enable the mouth cavity to expand greatly and allow the whale to take in vast quantities of water rich in plankton. When the mouth is almost completely shut, the lower part of the mouth cavity contracts again, pushing the tongue against the palate and forcing the water to gush out sideways. Instead of teeth, horny plates with fringed borders frame the upper jaw – the baleen or whalebone. These function as a sieve and trap the food – principally krill, a form of shrimp. Whalers have found up to two tons of krill in the stomach of a dead whale. The Blue Whale has neither a sense of smell nor acute vision, but has excellent hearing. As all whales, it can

identify objects by sending out precise cries and measuring the echoes. It breathes through its lungs and has two blowholes for nostrils on the top of the head. It surfaces every 10 to 15 minutes for air and its warm breath forms spray on contact with the cold air, sending a jet up to 20ft (6m) high. The name "Blue Whale" comes from its blue back and sides. After 10 to 11 months' gestation, the female produces one offspring measuring 23 – 26ft (7 – 8m) at birth and weighing up to 3 tons. The foetus increases by 15lb (7kg) a day from conception to birth. The young is suckled by its mother for six or seven months; the mother's udder muscles contract so that her milk can be pumped into the offspring's mouth. During the suckling period the mother produces an amount of milk equal to her own weight and loses a third of her weight in order to do this. At six to seven months the young measures 52ft (16m). As the period from concep-

tion to weaning takes 18 to 19 months, the female only produces every two years. A subspecies called the Pygmy Blue Whale (*Balaenoptera musculus brevicauda*) measures 66ft (20m) in length.

Geographic distribution. Atlantic, Pacific and Indian Oceans; more abundant in the Southern than the Northern Hemisphere. It is principally found in the southern part of the Indian Ocean.

Habitat. Oceanic. The Blue Whale migrates from the summer feeding grounds in the polar waters which are rich in plankton, with banks of krill up to 30ft (10m) wide, to their winter breeding grounds in temperate waters.

Population. The decline in numbers of the Blue Whale began in 1865 with the introduction of explosive harpoons fired from a cannon and with the advent of steam whaling-ships. This was accelerated by the development of the huge factory ships which can completely process the whale in one hour. Today, the species is rigidly protected by international law. Since 1969 the only whaling fleets operating in Antarctica have been those of the Soviet Union and Japan. The Soviets have since stopped. The world population of Blue Whales was probably between 200,000 and 300,000 of which 10,000 were the Pygmy subspecies. By 1963 this was reduced to 4,000. Today, thanks to complete protection, it is believed that numbers are increasing.

FIN WHALE OR COMMON RORQUAL

Balaenoptera physalus

CLASS
Mammals

SUBCLASS
Eutheria

ORDER
Cetacea

SUBORDER
Mysticeti

FAMILY
Balaenopteridae

GENUS
Balaenoptera

Description. The Fin Whale is the second largest animal after the Blue Whale. The average length is 60 – 80ft (18 – 24m) but some measure over 90ft (27m). This species is slimmer than other whales and swims very fast. The colouring is strangely asymmetrical: the dark colour on the back extends more towards the abdomen on the left side than on the right; the right mandible is a whitish colour on the outside and dark on the inside, while the left mandible is the opposite (detail below); the left half of the tongue is white. The throat and chest have the longitudinal furrows characteristic of all the Balaenopteridae. It has a similar reproductive cycle to the Blue Whale. The lifespan is more than 20 to 30 years. The Fin Whale enjoys leaping entirely out of the water, like Humpback Whales. Unlike other whales which live alone or in pairs, the Fin Whale lives in groups of 15 to 16 or even more. Like the Blue Whale its principal food is krill.

Geographic distribution. All oceans from the equatorial to the polar water.

Habitat. Fin Whales generally keep to the deep ocean waters, rarely approaching coastal waters.

Population. Intensive hunting, particularly in the course of this century, has notably reduced the numbers. It is estimated that the original world population was around 470,000 before exploitation started. By the 1980s it was increasing again from an all-time low of less than 100,000.

HUMPBACK WHALE
Megaptera novaeangliae

CLASS
Mammals

SUBCLASS
Eutheria

ORDER
Cetacea

SUBORDER
Mysticeti

FAMILY
Balaenopteridae

GENUS
Megaptera

Description. The Humpback Whale has a far more squat shape than other baleen whales. It measures up to 65ft (20m). The flippers are very large, about 3ft (1m) wide and 13 – 16ft (4 – 5m) long. Numerous cutaneous tubercles, some with bristles, cover the top of the head and jawbone; longitudinal furrows, characteristic of all rorquals, extend from throat to belly. In spite of its weight and huge bulk it is extremely agile and playful, leaping high out of the water like the dolphin, and diving back with an enormous splash. The Humpbacks are the most sonorous of the rorquals; when emitting air through their blowholes they produce a siren-like sound.

Geographic distribution. There are two populations throughout the oceans of the world – one in the Northern Hemisphere and the other in the Southern Hemisphere – with little exchange between them.

Habitat. Humpback Whales have a predilection for coastal waters, sometimes even venturing as far as the mouth of large rivers. They migrate seasonally from cold waters in winter to warm waters in summer where they reproduce.

Population. Agile and mobile, the Humpback was formerly the most difficult whale to hunt. It was not until this century, therefore, that their numbers rapidly declined. The original populations are believed to have been around 100,000 in the South and 150,000 in the North. Today they are fully protected. In the early 1980s the Humpback was still under 7,000 in total, though slowly increasing. Their coastal prevalence makes them prey to the dangers of pollution.

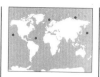

GREENLAND RIGHT WHALE OR BOWHEAD

Balaena mysticetus

CLASS
Mammals

SUBCLASS
Eutheria

ORDER
Cetacea

SUBORDER
Mysticeti

FAMILY
Balaenidae

GENUS
Balaena

Description. The Greenland Right Whale has an extraordinarily squat body. The head is one third of its total length. The mouth is huge, measuring 16 – 20ft (5 – 6m) long and 10ft (3m) wide, with enormous lips which cover the jawbone and "whale-bones." There are 300 – 360 whale-bones on each side and a single one can weigh 6½lb (3kg). The upper lip is distinctly arched. The blowholes are two narrow fissures measuring 18in (45cm) in length and are positioned on top of the head. The eyes, which see better underwater, are very small in proportion to the rest of the head and are directly over the corners of the jaw. The hearing pipes are directly behind the eyes. The edges of the jawbone are sparsely covered in short, white hairs. The tail fin is 6½ft (2m) long and 20 – 26ft (6 – 8m) wide; there is no dorsal fin. The species grows up to 66ft (20m) in length and weighs up to 83 tons. In common with other whales, a strip measuring 8 – 18in (20 – 45cm) of blubber lies under the smooth skin. The basic colour of the body is blue-black but adults have a grey-white patch on their chin. A similar species, and equally rare, is the Black Whale (*Eubalaena glacialis*) which is divided into three subspecies: the Basque, Japanese and Australian. In the Japanese subspecies, the Black Whale is up to 66ft (20m) long. The head, which is a quarter of the total length, is smaller than the Greenland Right Whale's. There are white areas on the skin due to barnacles; on the jawbone is a horny excrescence completely covered in small parasitic crustaceans. These whales belong to the genera *Balaena* and *Eubalaena* which are called Right Whales because, due to their huge bulk and slowness compared with the balaenopterids, they were the "right" whales to hunt when whalers pursued these great creatures in rowing boats.

Geographic distribution. The Greenland Right Whale is virtually confined to the Arctic Ocean in four isolated groups, though it has reappeared in the Sea of Japan where it was thought to be extinct. The Black Whale is found in the North Atlantic and northern Pacific as far as Taiwan.

Habitat. The Greenland Right Whale lives in arctic waters between huge icebergs that sometimes directly block its passage from one feeding ground to another. The Black Whale lives in temperate waters.

Population. The Greenland Right Whale was almost exterminated in the nineteenth century and has been fully protected since 1935, apart from a small number which are legally killed by Eskimos. It seems that they may now be increasing in the Pacific area and are slowly increasing in the Atlantic. The total population is put at a few thousand. The Black Whale has also been protected since 1935. This species was intensively hunted in the eighteenth and nineteenth centuries principally because of its presence in temperate waters, its high yield of oil and the fact that, once killed, the carcass floated. It is now increasing slowly, both in the western part of the North Atlantic and in the Southern Hemisphere. Despite their extreme rarity, Bowheads are killed, and even greater numbers injured, by Eskimos using explosive grenades. Despite international demands, the US government allows this destruction to continue.

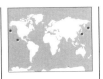

CLASS
Mammals

SUBCLASS
Eutheria

ORDER
Carnivora

SUBORDER
Fissipedia

FAMILY
Mustelidae

SUBFAMILY
Lutrinae

GENUS
Enhydra

SEA OTTER
Enhydra lutris

Description. Although smaller than the Giant Otter, the Sea Otter can be heavier, as its body, excluding the tail, is longer and more solid. A Sea Otter measuring 5 – 6ft (150 – 180cm) in length will weigh as much as 99lb (45kg). Its forefeet, which are small in proportion to the rest of its body, are webbed with short claws; the sole is hard and smooth. Its hind feet, which are placed fairly well back, are flipper-like with short claws; they are covered in fur. The fur varies in colour from reddish brown to black. It is diurnal, and most active at dawn and sunset. At night it rests in natural shelters along the rocky coastline, although in summer it often prefers floating seaweed away from the shore but in a safe position from sharks and whales – its natural enemies. Like other otters the Sea Otter is gregarious, remaining in family groups while on land – although never wandering far from the water's edge. The care shown between parents and offspring is remarkable: both male and female are warm and gentle towards the young and effusive exchanges of affection are common. There is no breeding season; copulation may occur at any time and females may be seen suckling pups throughout the year. A single pup is born (two are rare) and is reared by the mother with great care. When on land she carries the pup in her mouth; in water she swims on her back with the pup resting on her belly. The first swimming lessons are given by attentive parents, at any sign of danger, or tiredness on the pup's part, the mother carries her offspring to safety. The Sea Otter is mainly carnivorous and its diet is composed of sea urchins, molluscs, and shellfish (which it opens with stones as it floats on its back); it also eats a small amount of seaweed.

Geographic distribution. Once inhabited the whole of the Pacific coast from Japan to the Aleutian Islands and southwards to California. Today, only small restricted populations remain.

Habitat. Fairly steep rocky sea coasts and reefs close to the shore.

Population. They were hunted extensively for their valuable pelts and in 1911 their populations had dropped to between 1,000 and 2,000, and by 1920 the southern population was believed extinct. In 1938 a remnant population was discovered in southern California, which had increased to around 2,000 by the 1980s, while that of the Aleutians was estimated in the 1960s to be perhaps as high as 30,000. Thanks to strict protection and reintroduction programmes it continues to increase and spread.

MEDITERRANEAN MONK SEAL
Monachus monachus

CLASS
Mammals

SUBCLASS
Eutheria

ORDER
Carnivora

SUBORDER
Pinnipedae

FAMILY
Phocidae

SUBFAMILY
Monachinae

GENUS
Monachus

Description. There are three species of Monk Seal which all live in sub-tropical waters in the Northern Hemisphere, although each live in separate areas: *Monachus monachus* lives in the Mediterranean; *Monachus tropicalis* in the Caribbean; and *Monachus schauinslandi* on one of the Hawaiian Islands. The Monk Seal is the only hair seal which lives in a sub-tropical region. The name "monk" derives from its colouring which is uniformly dark over the back and white on the chest, vaguely resembling a monk's cowl. This pinniped has long strong nails on the front flippers while there are few or no nails on the back flippers. The Mediterranean Monk Seal is a large animal, larger than the common seal, and the male adult can grow up to 10ft (3m) in length. It can weigh more than 600lb (300kg). The female is smaller. This animal has a massive head with a short snout, large soft lips and long stiff whiskers. It has particularly large, luminous and expressive eyes. The limbs are short. The Mediterranean Monk Seal has a coat of short bristly hair, a yellowy-grey-brown colour on the back, which contrasts with the white on the chest and belly. The Monk Seal lives in small groups, preferably inside marine caves. The female gives birth to one young which is jet-black and weaned after six weeks.

Geographic distribution. The Monk Seal once lived along the Mediterrean coast, the Black Sea and north-western Africa as far as Cape Blanco and also around Madeira and the Canary Islands. Today, it exists only in the most remote Dodecanese Islands, and the Aegean Sea. It can also be found around Cape Blanco and the Mauritian coasts.

Habitat. Sea caves, particularly those with underwater entrances, which it finds on isolated islands or rocky coasts. It is not known whether the Monk Seal prefers to live in caves through choice or as a result of man's encroachment on its natural habitat.

Population. The Mediterranean Monk Seal is considered in grave danger of extinction. Its total population is less than 500. It has declined largely due to persecution by fishermen who see it as competition. Human population has developed near the coasts it inhabits, bringing with it pleasure boats and underwater swimming. The Monk Seal is protected in Italy, France, Yugoslavia, Greece and Bulgaria, but the law is difficult to enforce . In Africa it is protected by the African Convention of 1969. The last viable population in Greek waters is that centered on the Northern Sporades.

WALRUS
Odobenus rosmarus

Description. There are three subspecies of Walrus: the Arctic Walrus (*O. rosmarus rosmarus*), the Laptev Walrus (*O. rosmarus laptevi*), and the Pacific Walrus (*O. rosmarus divergens*). The total length of the adult male can occasionally exceed 13ft (4m); it can weigh up to 1½ tons. Females are generally smaller. They have protruding rootless upper canines, similar to long curved tusks which can be over 3ft (1m) long. Premolars and molars are smaller. On land they are awkward and clumsy; in the water they are agile and fast. Their diet consists mainly of crustaceans, molluscs, and even worms, which they dig up in the sand and mud, or scratch off rocks using their long tusks. They are gregarious animals and live in large herds which are subdivided into numerous family groups consisting of one adult male, two or three females, and a number of young. The gestation period is one year; a single young is born in April-May.

Geographic distribution. Arctic waters including Greenland and Hudson Bay. Today it has disappeared from the more southern areas. The Laptev Walrus is found along the northern coast of Siberia. The Pacific Walrus was found from the Bering Strait to the peninsula of Kamchatka and from Alaska to the Delphin Straits: it has also disappeared from more southern regions.

Habitat. Open sea during migration; sandy beaches off islands or continental coasts during reproduction.

Population. Under protection their numbers, like most other seals, can rebuild remarkably well. However, despite protection some populations appear to be declining. Hunting for tusks to supply carvers is one of the main threats.

DUGONG
Dugong dugon

CLASS
Mammals

SUBCLASS
Eutheria

ORDER
Sirenidae

FAMILY
Dugongidae

GENUS
Dugong

Description. The Dugong has a spindle-shaped body approximately 8 – 10ft (2.5 – 3.2m) long. It weighs between 310 – 440lb (140 – 200kg), but the adult male can reach up to 660lb (330kg). The head is large and rounded but indistinguishable from the neck. The mouth is very large and the fleshy lips are enormous with small bristly hairs. The male also has two incisors which, as the animal gets older, become very long and may even protrude beyond the lips. The front legs have developed, for the purpose of swimming, into two short spatula-shaped flippers. The skin varies in colour from brown to grey and is lighter on the belly; it is very thick, tough and completely hairless. The Dugong lives alone or in pairs, and very occasionally, in small family groups. After a gestation period of a year the female produces one young. The young is 5ft (1.5m) in length and is suckled while the mother holds it with her flippers. It is thought that ancient sailors, catching sight of these forms in the distance, believed they were sirens, hence the name now used in its classification.

Geographical distribution. Although enormously diminished in number, the Dugong still lives along the coast of the Red Sea and throughout the Indian Ocean.

Habitat. The Dugong is a typical marine-living mammal with a preference for warm, coastal waters. It lives on algae and aquatic plants. Occasionally it ventures to river mouths.

Population. Although not in immediate danger of extinction, the position of the Dugong is vulnerable: it is hunted throughout its range, and its numbers have diminished noticeably: it has even completely disappeared from many zones. The species is most numerous along the Australian coast and in New Guinea. It is hunted principally for its fat, its meat, and also its vestigial teeth. The Dugong is now protected in Australian waters (where a century ago it was relentlessly hunted) and in several other countries.

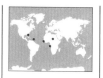

MANATEE
Trichechus manatus

CLASS
Mammals

SUBCLASS
Eutheria

ORDER
Sirenidae

FAMILY
Trichechidae

GENUS
Trichechus

Description. This animal has a spindle-shaped body and a smaller, squarer head than the Dugong. The thick, upper lip is split and each half can move independently of the other. The body is sparsely covered with bristles. The tail is very large and flat and not forked as in the Dugong. The skin is 2in (5cm) thick and varies in colour from grey to brown. It can grow up to 15ft (4.50m) in length and weigh about 7cwt (680kg), but normally sizes vary between 300 – 800lb (140 – 360kg). After a gestation period of five to six months one young is born (sometimes two) which is about 3ft (1m) long. The birth takes place underwater, but the mother immediately brings the new born pup to the surface. The pup stays with its mother for about two years and is suckled for 18 months.

Geographic distribution. The West Indian Manatee used to inhabit all of the coastal waters of the Americas; now it is limited to Florida, the West Indies, the Atlantic coast along Mexico, and the northern coast of South America. The Amazonian Manatee inhabits the Amazon and Orinoco upper river basins. The West African Manatee inhabits the rivers and creeks along the west coast of Africa.

Habitat. The shallow coastal waters of bays and estuaries, occasionally lagoons and rivers where the current is slow. They feed on aquatic plants and algae.

Population. Manatees have been intensively hunted throughout their range for their meat, fat, and tough hides. They have also suffered as a result of the polluted coastal waters of America. Although it is protected in the United States and several other countries, numbers continue to decline. In Florida, a large number are killed every year by motor-boat propellers. There are about 1,000 Manatees in the United States and several thousand more throughout the countries it inhabits. Those at the northern limits of their range are occasionally killed by prolonged cold weather.

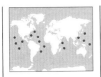

LEATHERBACK TURTLE
Dermochelys coriacea

Description. This is the largest living turtle and is distinguished from all others by the particular structure of its carapace, which has no horny plates and is formed of small boney plaques, joined together in a mosaic pattern, and embedded in the extremely strong, leathery skin. It reaches a length of 6½ft (2m) and weighs 1,540lb (700kg).
Geographic distribution. Temperate and tropical zones; the eggs are only laid in the latter.
Habitat. Marine.
Population. The Leatherback Turtle is a critically endangered species. Although they are generally not eaten, their eggs are prized. Many die after ingesting plastic bags and other floating refuse which they confuse for jellyfish, their main diet. Others perish in fishing nets. They are protected in most parts of their range.

HAWKSBILL TURTLE
Eretmochelys imbricata

Description. The Hawksbill Turtle is fairly small, with a shell measuring about 2ft (60 cm). It has large, variegated yellow and brown scales. The horny sheath on the upper jaw forms a beak similar to a bird of prey. It is omnivorous.
Geographic distribution. Mediterranean (although it has disappeared from a few areas); the Atlantic, Pacific, and Indian Oceans. The eggs are laid only in warm regions: South America, Africa, Australia, and southern Asia.
Habitat. Shallow coastal waters.
Population. The Hawksbill Turtle has been hunted extensively for its shell which was used for tortoise shell items such as combs and ornamental articles. It was hoped that the invention of plastic would stop the hunting. However, it is now hunted for its flesh which is used as a substitute for Green Turtle in turtle soup. In addition, many are drowned in fishing nets, and breeding beaches suffer from disturbance. Protection will have to be more stringent to save it from extinction.

EXTINCT ANIMALS

AUROCHS
Bos primigenius

This wild ox (right) was once found in all the temperate zones of the world; from Europe to North Africa, Asia Minor, northern India, and China. It has been extinct since the seventeenth century and was last seen in the wild in central Europe. Its extinction was probably due to the gradual disappearance of wooded areas and the subsequent loss of its food source. The male was about 10ft (3m) in length and 6ft (1.85m) in height. It weighed up to one ton. Females were smaller. The horns could measure up to 32 in (80cm) in length. Males were brown and females and young a rusty colour.

TARPAN
Equus gmelini

The Tarpan had a grey coat with a broad dark stripe running down its spine. The coat grew longer during the winter months. It was once found on the southern Russian plains and in the scrubland of central and eastern Europe. The species became extinct between the eighteenth and nineteenth centuries when its habitat was transformed and it became persecuted by horse-breeders who found that male Tarpans polluted their stock. The last surviving Tarpan died in 1879. Similar strains of wild horses were found in Germany and Poland. These have been successfully bred and a small group released into the Bialowiecza forest in Poland.

BLUEBUCK
Hippotragus leucophaeus

The only information we have about the Bluebuck has been left to us by nineteenth-century explorers and settlers in South Africa. This small antelope had a blue-grey coat with a brown chest.

Females were considerably smaller. The Bluebuck had long graceful curving horns. It was once found in a restricted area in South Africa but was killed by the early Boer settlers. It was only officially described for the first time in 1766; the description was based on a stuffed example in Leiden Museum, Holland. The last Bluebuck was killed in 1799.

GIANT MOA
Dinornis maximus

The Giant Moa was a huge bird which grew up to 10ft (3m) in height and weighed 550lb (250kg). Similar to the ostrich, the Giant Moa had a small head with a long curved neck. It had massive toes and no wings (there is no trace of them on the skeleton). The Giant Moa was exclusive to New Zealand and fed off grasses, berries, and seeds. They became extinct through hunting (Maoris hunted it for its meat, bones and eggs), and from the transformation of its habitat. The species became extinct between the tenth and seventeenth centuries; the last Pygmy Moa (*Megalopteryx didinus*) possibly died in 1773.

BARBARY LION
Panthera leo leo

The Barbary Lion was once widespread throughout the African continent apart from the central Sahara and humid tropical forests. It was also found across Asia from the Arabian peninsula to India. It was a huge beast over 3ft (1m) tall and the male had an enormous thick mane which covered the head, neck, chest, and belly. It lived principally in the coastal regions and around oases where there was plenty of vegetation. The ancient Romans whose dominion extended over North Africa used to capture these lions for their cruel public games in arenas. Local tribesmen also killed the beasts. When the European armies occupied North Africa they continued to slaughter the lions for food or captured them for circuses. The last Barbary Lion was killed in Morocco in 1920. Many generations of lions retaining their basic characteristics have been bred in captivity.

QUAGGA
Equus quagga

The Quagga was a species of Plains Zebra which interbred with Burchell's Zebra (*Equus burchelli*). Its name came from its characteristic cry which sounded like "qua-ha." The Quagga had brown and white stripes only on the head, neck, and shoulders. A brown-black stripe extended down its back as far as the tail. It once inhabited the great plains of South Africa where it roamed in herds. Even at the beginning of the nineteenth century this species was numerous throughout its range. It was slaughtered by the Boer settlers for its meat and hides. The last Quagga was killed in the wild in 1878. There had been a number in European zoos but the last one died in Amsterdam Zoo in 1883. All that remains of the Quagga are a few stuffed examples and photographs. If there had been any notion of wildlife conservation at that time it would probably have survived.

DODO
Raphus cucullatus

The Dodo (below) was a very large flightless bird. It had a strong curved beak and a massive fleshy head. Its eyes were placed well forward and it had remarkable vision. It fed on leaves, berries, hard fruit, and snails which it broke with its powerful beak. The Dodo was found on Mauritius in the Indian Ocean living in shrubby forest where there was plenty of food. When the Portuguese arrived in the sixteenth century the Dodo was fairly numerous. In the first half of the seventeenth century a number of examples were taken to Europe. These strange-looking harmless birds and their nestlings were easy prey for the rats and livestock that were introduced to the island by the Portuguese. By 1681 it had become extinct.

CAROLINA PARAKEET

Conuropsis carolinensis

This beautiful North American parakeet has been extinct since 1914. It had green and yellow plumage with pink cheeks and forehead. There were two subspecies: the Carolina and the Lousiana Parakeets. They lived in woodland in the southern half of the United States and were killed for meat and feathers. By 1880 numbers had declined drastically and attempts were made to protect them; but it was already too late. The last Louisiana Parakeets were killed in 1912 and the last Carolina Parakeet died in Cincinnati Zoo in 1914.

STELLER'S SEA COW

Hydrodamalis gigas

Steller's Sea Cow (below) could grow up to 26ft (8m) in length and weigh four tons. It had no teeth and had a tough grey-brown skin which was covered in crustaceans. It lived exclusively on Bering Island and other islands of the small group of the Commodores in the Bering Sea. It grazed on algae and aquatic grasses in shallow waters. It was discovered in 1741 by Georg Wilhelm Steller, a botanist on an expedition led by the Dane, Vitus Behring. They were shipwrecked off Bering Island and were forced to remain there over winter. Steller studied these sea cows and published his findings. Soon after hunters came to these islands in search of sea otters for their valuable fur. They discovered that Steller's Sea Cow was easy prey and had edible flesh. Within a few years they had wiped out the entire species. The last one was killed in 1768.

PASSENGER PIGEON

Ectopistes migratorius

This bird was probably at one time one of the most common in North America. It was an elegant-looking pigeon which lived in enormous flocks. It ate seeds,

nuts and berries. The Passenger Pigeon was widely distributed throughout northeast America. In autumn they migrated south as far as Mexico. They lived in vast woodlands; once the land was cultivated by early settlers they caused untold damage. Up until 1850 one could see huge clouds consisting of millions of Passenger Pigeons. These huge flocks were decimated by hunting: either with cudgels or rifles. Its meat was one of the main food sources in the United States and they were exported to Europe. Towards the end of the nineteenth century hardly any Passenger Pigeons could be seen. In 1900 the last Passenger Pigeon in the wild was killed in Ohio. The last one in captivity died in Cincinnati Zoo in 1914.

THYLACINE
Thylacinus cynocephalus

The Thylacine or Tasmanian Pouched Wolf was also known as the Tasmanian Tiger because of the stripes across its back. It was the largest of all the carnivorous marsupials about the size of a large dog and similar in appearance. Females had a pouch which opened backwards. The Thylacine was once widely distributed in Australia and New Guinea. A mummified carcass found in a cave in western Australia was carbon-dated at between 2940 and 2340 BC. They became extinct there by about 1000 BC. and only survived in Tasmania. They were massacred remorselessly from the mid nineteenth century because of their threat to domestic livestock. They were last positively recorded in the 1930s and allegedly sighted in recent years which was unsubstantiated. The last surviving animal died in Hobart Zoo in 1933 and they had never reproduced in captivity.

ELEPHANT BIRD
Aepyornis maximus

Similar to the ostrich, the Elephant Bird was possibly the largest bird on earth, measuring up to 11ft (3.50m) in height and weighing 1,100lb (500kg). It had a long neck, small atrophied wings, and massive legs. Its enormous eggs were over 1ft (30cm) long. The Elephant Bird was exclusive to Madagascar and was forced into inaccessible forest in the south of the island. It was hunted for its meat and probably became extinct in the second half of the seventeenth century. There is a skeleton in a museum in Paris.

GREAT AUK
Pinguinis impennis

This flightless bird was an excellent swimmer whose wings had become adapted for water. The Great Auk inhabited the islands and coasts of the North Atlantic. It travelled in large groups. In 1534 the French explorer, Jacques Cartier, landed on Funk Island off Newfoundland where he saw a large number of Great Auks. It was the original "pinguin" and sailors used the name for similar-looking birds in the southern oceans. Within half an hour of landing Cartier and his sailors had slaughtered enough to fill two rowing boats. It was killed for its meat, feathers, and fat. Within three centuries the Great Auk had disappeared. This was also partially due to volcanic activity which destroyed the last nesting territories. The last Great Auks were killed in 1844 off Iceland. A number of stuffed examples exist.

BIBLIOGRAPHY

GENERAL

Day, David, *The Doomsday Book of Animals*, Viking Press, New York, 1981

Fisher, J., Simon, N. & Vincent, J., *The Red Book Wildlife in Danger*, Collins, London, 1969

Sitwell, Nigel, *The Shell Guide to Britain's Threatened Wildlife*, Collins, London, 1984

MAMMALS

Allen, G.M., *Extinct and Vanishing Mammals of the Western Hemisphere*, Cooper Square, New York, 1942 (rp. 1972)

Burt, W.H., *A Field Guide to the Mammals*, Houghton-Mifflin, Boston, 1964

Burton, John A., *Collins Guide to Rare Mammals of the World*, Collins, London, 1987

Chapman, Joseph A. & Feldhamer, George A., *Wild Mammals of North America*, Johns Hopkins University Press, Baltimore, 1982

Marlow Basil, J., *Marsupials of Australia*, Jacaranda Wiley Ltd., Brisbane, 1962

Nowak, Ronald M. & Paradiso, John, L., *Walker's Mammals of the World* (4th ed.), Johns Hopkins University Press, Baltimore & London, 1983

Whitaker, John O. Jr., *The Audubon Society Field Guide to North American Mammals*, Knopf, New York, 1980

BIRDS

King, W.B., *Endangered Birds of the World. The ICBP Bird Red Data Books*, Smithsonian Institution Press and ICBP, Washington, 1981

Forshaw, J.M., *Parrots of the World*, Lansdowne Press, London, 1973

Mountfort, Guy, *Rare Birds of the World*, Collins, London, 1988

REPTILES

Bellairs, A., *The Life of Reptiles*, Vols 1-2, Weidenfeld & Nicolson, London, 1969

Duellman, W.E., and Trueb, L., *Biology of Amphibians*, McGraw-Hill Book Company, New York, 1985

Frost D. (ed.), *Amphibian Species of the World*, Association of Systematics Collections and Allen Press, Lawrence, 1984

Groombridge, B., *The IUCN Amphibia-Reptilia Red Data Book. 1. Testudines Crocodylia Rhynchocephalia*, IUCN, Gland, 1982

Perrero, L., *Alligators and Crocodiles of the World. The Disappearing Dragons*, Windward Publ. Inc., Miami, 1975

PERIODICALS/JOURNALS

AAZPA Newsletter, American Association of Zoological Parks and Aquariums, Wheeling, West Virginia

International Zoo News, Zoo-Centrum, London

Oryx, Journal of the Fauna and Flora Preservation Society, London

Wildlife Conservation, New York Zoological Society, New York,

World Wildlife News, WWF, Horsham, UK

FURTHER READING AND INFORMATION

Within the past decade there has been an enormous surge of interest in wildlife conservation and this is reflected in the huge increase in the books available. The bibliography is not intended to be complete, but aims to give the general reader guidance in seeking more detailed information. The specialist researcher will need to consult one of the many computerized data-bases or bibliographic systems.

RED DATA BOOKS

The concept of the Red Data Book was the brainchild of the late Sir Peter Scott, and since the mid 1960s an increasing number of them have been published for groups of both animals and plants and also for regions and countries. They are essentially listings of threatened species with their degrees of threat indicated, though many of the Red Data Books are also effectively detailed monographs of the species concerned.

IUCN/ICBP RED DATA BOOKS

The International Union for Conservation of Nature and Natural Resources (IUCN) and the International Council for Bird Preservation (ICBP) publish a wide range of books and pamphlets concerning endangered wildlife, including the international Red Data Books, and Action Plans for many groups of threatened plants and animals. Any serious student of endangered species will need to read some of their publications.

ICBP

32 Cambridge Road
Cambridge CB3 0PJ
UK

IUCN

219c Huntingdon Road
Cambridge CB3 0DL
UK

Catalogues of their publications may be obtained by writing to them.

INDEX

INDEX

INDEX

INDEX

INDEX

INDEX